T3-BIF-936

EVERYDAY
UBUNTU

LIVING BETTER TOGETHER,
THE AFRICAN WAY

To the person I admire most –
Mom, you are a gift to the world
and to me

EVERYDAY UBUNTU

LIVING BETTER TOGETHER, THE AFRICAN WAY

MUNGI NGOMANE

appetite
by RANDOM HOUSE

Copyright © 2019 Nompumelelo Mungi Ngomane
Illustrations copyright © Hanlie Burger: www.amafu.co.za

All rights reserved. The use of any part of this publication,
reproduced, transmitted in any form or by any means, electronic,
mechanical, photocopying, recording, or otherwise, or stored in a
retrieval system, without the prior written consent of the publisher—
or, in case of photocopying or other reprographic copying, license
from the Canadian Copyright Licensing Agency—is an infringement
of the copyright law.

Appetite by Random House® and colophon are registered
trademarks of Penguin Random House LLC.

First published in Great Britain in 2019 by Bantam Press,
an imprint of Transworld Publishers

Library and Archives Canada Cataloguing in Publication
is available upon request.
ISBN: 9780525610991
eBook ISBN: 9780525611004

Text designed by Hampton and set in Avenir
Case design by Marianne Issa El-Khoury/TW
Case prints by Hanlie Burger © amafu.co.za
Case typeface Mr Eaves Sans © Emigre Foundry
Printed and bound in China

Published in Canada by Appetite by Random House®,
a division of Penguin Random House Canada Limited.

www.penguinrandomhouse.ca

10 9 8 7 6 5 4 3 2 1

appetite
by RANDOM HOUSE

Penguin
Random
House

CONTENTS

FOREWORD

I am sure most parents can attest to the pride they feel when they hear or see their child pass on something she or he has learned from them. We remember how that same child reacted initially when we taught them the lesson in question or showed them how their behaviour was not something to be proud of – that they knew better. We remember the pout, the anger at being corrected or encouraged to do and be better.

'But he said it first,' or 'But she took my toy first!' Words of defence and justification. Here is your daughter or son, however, teaching that very lesson to your grandchild, showing that what you said many years ago – the teaching – has not been ignored or even forgotten; that the words were taken in and continue to guide. That the wisdom is now being imparted to the next generation.

We feel pride, and some relief, to know that the wisdom we too received from those who came before us is being passed on. Maybe that is all we can hope for – that one generation will make sure the next knows how we are meant to live as human beings, caring for one another and respecting each other's humanity. I am sure, then, that those of you who are parents and grandparents can imagine my joy in being asked to introduce a book by my granddaughter, Mungi, about a principle that has been central to my teachings to my children and our larger community.

Ubuntu is a concept that, in my community, is one of the most fundamental aspects of living lives of courage, compassion and connection. It is one that I cannot remember not knowing about. I understood from early on in my life that being known as a person with *ubuntu* was one of the highest accolades one could ever receive. Almost daily we were encouraged to show it in our relations with family, friends and strangers alike. I have often said that the idea and practice of *ubuntu* is one of Africa's greatest gifts to the world. A gift with which, unfortunately, not many in the world are familiar. The lesson of *ubuntu* is best described in a proverb that is found in almost every African language, whose translation is, 'A person is a person through other persons.' The fundamental meaning of the proverb is that everything we learn and experience in the world is through our relationships with other people. We are therefore called to examine our actions and thoughts, not just for what they will achieve for us, but for how they impact on others with whom we are in contact.

At its most simple, the teaching of this proverb and of *ubuntu* is similar to the Golden Rule found in most faith teachings: 'Do unto others as you would have them do unto you!' But one who has *ubuntu* goes a step beyond that. It is not only our actions we are called to keep track of, but our very being in the world. How we live, talk and walk in the world is as much a statement of our character as our actions. One with *ubuntu* is careful to walk in the world as one who recognizes the infinite worth of everyone with whom he or she comes into contact. So it is not simply a way of behaving, it is indeed a way of being!

Everyday Ubuntu offers the reader a chance to reflect on the ways in which the practice of *ubuntu* can help us to be someone in the world who builds bridges, someone who sees each interaction as a chance to foster a more positive environment. The stories that Mungi shares are ones we can all relate to at one level or another. They are the everyday opportunities and challenges we are given to live in the world with *ubuntu*. On any given day, we are each offered many chances to be the person who – whether it be through words, actions, or even silence and inaction – offers space to those we encounter to experience care and relationship.

I am both proud and happy to be able to encourage you to read a book that introduces a philosophy that has meant so much to me, written by my own granddaughter. I believe that it will open your eyes, minds and hearts to a way of being in the world that will make it a better and more caring one.

God's richest blessings.

Archbishop Desmond Tutu
Cape Town, South Africa
May 2019

I AM ONLY BECAUSE YOU ARE

'When we want to give high praise to someone we say, "Yhu, u nobuntu": 'Hey, so-and-so has ubuntu." Then you are generous, you are hospitable, you are friendly and caring and compassionate.'

Archbishop Desmond Tutu,
No Future Without Forgiveness

***Ubuntu* is a way of life from which we can all learn. And it's one of my favourite words. In fact, my feelings about *ubuntu* run so deeply that I've had it tattooed on the inside of my right wrist. For me, it's a small word but it encapsulates a huge idea. Originating from a Southern African philosophy, it encompasses all our aspirations about how to live life well, together. We feel it when we connect with other people and share a sense of humanity; when we listen deeply and experience an emotional bond; when we treat ourselves and other people with the dignity they deserve.**

It exists when people unite for a common good, and in today's chaotic and often confusing world, its values are more important than ever because it says that if we join together we can overcome our differences and our problems. Whoever we are, wherever we live, whatever our culture, *ubuntu* can help us co-exist in harmony and peace.

I was raised in a community that taught me *ubuntu* as one of my earliest lessons. My grandfather, Archbishop Desmond Tutu, explained the essence of *ubuntu* as, 'My humanity is caught up, is inextricably bound up, in yours.'

In my family, we were brought up to understand that a person who has *ubuntu* is one whose life is worth emulating. The bedrock of the philosophy is respect, for yourself and for others. So if you're able to see other people, even strangers, as fully human you will never be able to treat them as disposable or without worth.

Life in today's complex societies is full of trials and tribulations, and there are self-help books aplenty attempting to guide us through it. We are told to meditate and reflect; to look inside ourselves for answers, as that is the only place we will find them. The notion of 'self-care' is a whole movement in itself.

There is certainly a time and place for self-examination. However, *ubuntu* teaches us to also look *outside* ourselves to find answers. It's about seeing the bigger picture; the other side of the story. *Ubuntu* is about reaching out to our fellow men and women, through whom we might just find the comfort, contentment and sense of belonging we crave. *Ubuntu* tells us that individuals are nothing without other human beings. It encompasses everyone, regardless of race, creed or colour. It embraces our differences and celebrates them.

The concept of *ubuntu* is found in almost all African Bantu languages. It shares its roots with the word 'bantu' – meaning 'people' – and almost always denotes the importance of community and connection. The idea of *ubuntu* is best represented in both Xhosa and Zulu by the proverb '*umuntu, ngumuntu, ngabantu*', meaning 'a person is a person through other persons'. It is a proverb which exists in all the African languages of South Africa. The word '*ubuntu*', or closely related words, are found in many other African countries and cultures.

In Rwanda and Burundi it means 'human generosity'.

In parts of Kenya '*utu*' is a concept, which means that every action should be for the benefit of the community.

In Malawi it's '*uMunthu*', an idea that on your own you are no better than a wild animal, but two or more people make a community.

The sense that 'I am only because you are' runs throughout.

My grandfather coined the term 'Rainbow Nation' for South Africa after the country's first democratic elections in 1994, to symbolize the unity of its cultures after the collapse of apartheid. In this book you will find fourteen lessons built on *ubuntu*, which is the same number of chapters as there are in the Rainbow Nation's constitution.

Ubuntu is the founding principle of my grandfather's life work and, as a patron of the Tutu Foundation UK myself, I too aspire to live by its teachings in my everyday life. By introducing this philosophy to you, I hope it enhances your life experience as much as it has enhanced mine. I hope it encourages you to reach out to the people around you – both friends and strangers – who make you who you are.

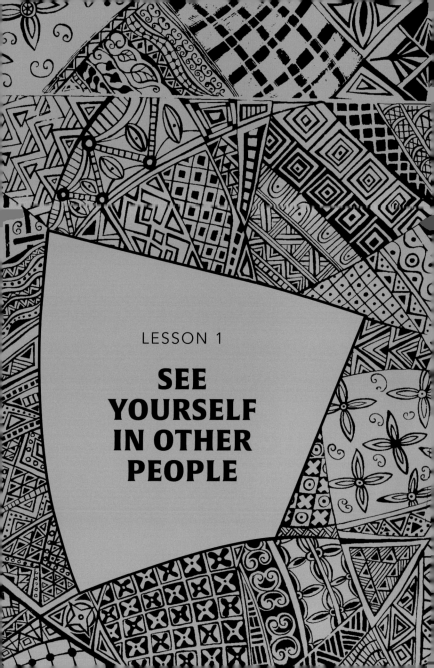

LESSON 1

SEE
YOURSELF
IN OTHER
PEOPLE

'Sawubona!'

A South African greeting, meaning 'I
see you!'

If we are able to see ourselves in other people, our experience in the world will inevitably be a richer, kinder, more connected one. If we look at others and see ourselves reflected back, we inevitably treat people better.

This is *ubuntu*.

Ubuntu shouldn't be confused with kindness, however. Kindness is something we might try to show more of, but *ubuntu* goes much deeper. It recognizes the inner worth of every human being – starting with yourself.

Ubuntu guided the struggle against apartheid, a harsh and institutionalized system of racial segregation in South Africa where, until 1994, black and white people were forced to lead completely separate lives. The anti-apartheid movement was never an 'anti-white' struggle but instead was a struggle for *all* South Africans, to be seen and treated as equal. If you can face adversity and oppression, and hold on to *ubuntu* and live it in your daily life, you will experience the best way to overcome division. It's South Africa's gift to the world.

I am grateful to have been brought up around lots of wise people. My mother, Nontombi Naomi Tutu, is a peace activist, feminist, public speaker and, recently, an ordained priest. My grandparents were at the forefront of the anti-apartheid movement and my grandfather won a Nobel Peace Prize in 1984 for his non-violent struggle against the system. Soaking up my family's words, experiences, laughter and beliefs has helped me on my own life's journey. Much of how they live epitomizes the spirit of *ubuntu*, with service to others viewed as a priority.

SHARE THE JOURNEY

The anti-apartheid struggle in South Africa was a response to the colonization and oppression of black, coloured and Asian South Africans. Thousands of people lost their lives, violence tore the country apart, and it took many years to recover. It ended in 1994 with the nation's first democratic elections, though even today South Africa struggles to overcome the impact of apartheid.

Back in December 1984, my grandfather flew to Norway to receive his Nobel Prize. As a priest, he was committed to finding justice through non-violent means while at the same time highlighting the pain and inequality of apartheid to the world. He wanted everyone to know about its costs to all South Africans.

The Nobel committee told prize recipients they could invite as many people as they wanted to the ceremony at the University of Oslo, and my grandfather took this offer seriously. He extended the invitation to his immediate and wider family, and lots of other guests, until there were at least fifty people on his list. These friends travelled from all over the world – South Africa, the United States, Lesotho and the United Kingdom. They were people my grandfather had known throughout his life and with whom he'd shared his journey.

That evening there was a bomb scare and the university hall had to be evacuated. Eventually, once it was safe to return to the building, my grandfather walked up to the stage to collect his award. He paused to look out over the crowd. It was then that a profound thought struck him. This nomination had happened *because of all these other people in the room*. That moment crystallized the realization that everything he had achieved in his life had been as a result of others and their help.

Afterwards, it was time to celebrate, but even though everyone – including the King of Norway – had returned to the hall, the musicians had left for the day. So my grandfather's South African guests stepped in to provide the singing, and once again made their presence even more appreciated.

Ubuntu tells us we are *only* who we are thanks to other people. Of course we have our parents to credit for bringing us into the world, but beyond this there are hundreds – if not thousands – of relationships, big and small, along the way, which teach us something about life and how to live it well. Our parents or guardians teach us how to walk and talk. Our teachers at school teach us how to read and write. A mentor might help us find fulfilling work. A lover might teach us emotional lessons, both good and bad – we learn from all experiences. Every interaction will have brought us to where we are today.

However, in the West we are also taught that it's a badge of honour to claim to be self-made. We applaud those whom we perceive as having achieved fame and fortune through their own efforts, happy to overlook the fact that nothing can be achieved in a vacuum. We are further taught that competition leads to self-fulfilment and progress, even though pitting yourself against others leads to unhelpful comparisons and a grinding sense of not being enough.

How often have you compared your own life to someone else's and felt *worse off*? How often do you crave more, however much you already have? A bigger house. More money. More work, more time off.

The rise of social media has played a major role in stoking our fires of discontent. Whenever we scroll through Facebook or Instagram, we are looking at carefully curated windows into people's lives. Images are often edited and reshot to look as appealing as possible. Smiling happy families in immaculate rooms, celebrations, a new job announcement, a new kitchen, a new relationship.

However wonderful it is to celebrate the good things in our friends' lives, many of us also follow hundreds sometimes thousands – of strangers who appear to live lives that are richer, more fun and shinier than our own. These are people who we don't know personally but who influence what we long to buy, the way we feel and our aspirations. The subtext is that an 'influencer' is a better person than the ordinary person.

Ubuntu teaches us the opposite of this and says that absolutely everyone on this earth is of equal value because our humanity is what matters the most. Instead of comparing ourselves to others, we should value other people's contributions to our day-to-day lives. There are some influencers who can have a positive effect on us, though. I no longer use social media and have little access to influencers, but the ones I do have access to – through podcasts – focus on providing their audiences with good content rather than monetizing. They share messages, interviews and advice on a range of topics including mental health, wellness, relationships and careers.

Think about who has made you into the person you are today. Take a moment to consider all the people who help you in your life. Parents and friends will be on the list, but try widening the circle. Perhaps there are more people on your list than you've ever thought about before? The mechanic who fixes your car so you can have a weekend away. The barista who lets it slide when you're a few pennies short paying for your morning coffee. The person who lets you off the train first because you're clearly in a hurry. All these seemingly meaningless interactions help you move more smoothly through life. These people's actions can make a difference to your day, just as you can make a difference to other people's with yours.

Think about the people you help. Write a second list. The friend who asks you for advice. The colleague you help with a task at work. The child you nurture by cooking and caring for them every day. The loved one who needs a shoulder to cry on.

Notice how life is about give and take. Do you enjoy giving more than taking? What have you done for someone that made you feel good about yourself? And what can you do today, or tomorrow?

YOU ARE ENOUGH

With eyes imbued with *ubuntu* we view our world via a prism not only of equality but also of gratitude. We aspire not to be unduly influenced by others when we form our thoughts and feelings, but we also acknowledge everyone who has helped us to become who we are. The parents who give us space and freedom to experiment with our lives, the teachers and mentors who offer their wisdom for our journeys, the friends who encourage us, or the family members who might have loaned us money. We feel grateful for where we are, right here and right now, as *ubuntu* teaches us we are *enough*. We don't need to compare our lives to others' and what they may or may not have in them. Instead, we can be grateful for other people's contributions to ours.

With *ubuntu* in our lives we can choose to view others as our equals, seeing them as we would want others to see us. All too often we observe only the role people play in the world and think nothing more of them. *Ubuntu* tells us that we are no better or worse than anyone else. Everyone deserves to be treated with humanity.

We can look into the eyes of somebody begging on the street and feel compassion rather than judgement. We can thank someone who cleans toilets rather than look down on them for the service they provide.

Ubuntu refutes the notion that a person can ever be self-made, because we are all interconnected. We should not be fooled by the myth of the self-made individual, as no one exists in true isolation. In the words of the poet John Donne: 'No man is an island.'

The antithesis of _ubuntu_ is the belief that greed, selfishness and rugged individualism will provide everything you need to get ahead in life. We often hear that we'll need to stand on the heads of others to reach our goals. The workplace in particular can be ruthless and the Darwinian notion of survival of the fittest is still the rule of thumb for many people.

I've often heard my elders say that those who do ill towards others might think that they personally don't suffer any negative consequences from their actions, but if you look deeper, the harm to the ill-doer is there to be seen.

Under apartheid, for example, at first glance segregation afforded white South Africans lives of privilege. They lived separately, in well-built communities. They had access to better education and healthcare than their black counterparts. However, these privileges came at a great cost to their freedom. They gave up many rights for the privilege of power when they were taught to live in fear of black people. They built high walls around their homes and they trapped themselves in gated communities, afraid to leave. They became prisoners in circumstances of their own making.

ASK YOURSELF: HOW CAN YOU SEE YOURSELF IN OTHER PEOPLE?

It can be tricky to give a direct and concise translation of *ubuntu* in English. However, Nelson Mandela explained its essence in a TV interview with South African journalist Tim Modise in 2006. In simple terms (see opposite) he described what *ubuntu* meant to him.

We all want to belong. It's human nature to have tribes (friends, loved ones, work colleagues, exercise buddies . . .), but more than ever we also need to learn to live and work together with everyone, including strangers. Reaching outside of ourselves can give us what we need to feel fulfilled inside. Seeing your fellow men and women as your allies (from the Latin '*alligare*', meaning 'to bind to') serves us all. Seeing yourself in other people is a powerful force for good.

'In the old days, when we were young, a traveller through a country would stop at a village, and he didn't have to ask for food or water; once he stops, the people give him food, entertain him.

That is one aspect of *ubuntu*, but it will have various aspects. *Ubuntu* does not mean that people should not address themselves. The question therefore is, what are you going to do in order to enable the community around you, and enable it to improve? These are important things in life. And if you can do that, you have done something very important.'

Nelson Mandela

Connect mindfully with strangers. We can all be distracted, heavily preoccupied and feel there is never enough time to do everything we either want to do or feel the need to do. We might think there's no need to say a genuine thank-you to the shop owner who has just served us, or we might be looking at our phone as the guard on the train checks our ticket. We might not notice when someone is holding open a door for us, or steps out of the way to let us through. Try to look everyone you come across in the eye. Connect with them. Smile. Say thank you with enthusiasm. Notice how this makes you feel and how the interactions you have with others change for the better.

Notice your judgements, feel them, and quietly let them go. We all make judgements, consciously or subconsciously, all the time. You might find yourself looking at a person living on the street and wonder whether they'll spend the money you've given them on drugs. You might hear a screaming child on a bus and wonder whether the mother or father is a good parent. You might worry the young person wearing a hoodie and walking towards you is up to no good and cross the road to avoid them.

However, when we pass judgement on other people we become blind and limit our own opportunities. Judgements serve no purpose other than to cast others into roles that are likely to be inaccurate, as you create a narrative with no foundation in truth. Judging others shuts down our capacity for compassion and increases our isolation. We all do it, but *ubuntu* tells us it won't bring joy. For one day, try to observe without judgement and quietly let negative thoughts go.

LESSON 2

STRENGTH LIES IN UNITY

'If you want to go quickly, go
alone. If you want to go far, go
together.'

African proverb

'Sticks in a bundle are
unbreakable.'

Bondei proverb

Ubuntu rejects the notion that any human being can ever be entirely self-made because no person can exist in isolation. *I am only because you are*. However, it also goes further and highlights the incredible power we can harness if we choose to stand together.

'United we stand, divided we fall' is a phrase that's been used through the ages to inspire unity, from the Ancient Greeks to the founding fathers of the United States of America, and at political rallies from London to Cape Town. Yet it's easy to forget the potential we have as a collective. Apathy and isolation have sometimes led us to think our contribution to causes we believe in has no value. However, we all have a voice. And it's loudest when it's expressed alongside the voices of others. There is always strength in numbers.

MAKE UNITY A PRIORITY

From a young age we are encouraged to think as individuals and focus on our own achievements; to look out for 'number one'. Many of us then go on to spend our adult working lives in silence in front of a computer screen, secluded in a cubicle, or in a job where there's little time or culture for face-to-face conversations. The digital revolution has reduced our capacity to see and speak to other human beings in the flesh. We have become virtual rather than physical beings. We don't make phone calls any more, we message people. We don't arrange meetings, we send emails instead.

This lack of human contact is in direct contrast to the African way of life, where cooperation is vital to enduring hostile conditions. When you need to survive by living off the same land as your neighbour and working alongside them, collaboration is key.

'It takes a village to raise a child' is believed to be an African proverb that stems from the understanding that a unified community is a strong community. Every single person counts, everyone contributes, and by working together great things can happen.

WEALTH DOESN'T EQUATE TO WORTH

Our need to seek out bonds with other humans hasn't changed since time began – we are by nature social animals – but the emphasis on the importance of social interactions has changed beyond recognition. Society largely values those with a higher socioeconomic standing so, as a consequence, many of us strive to achieve goals relating to money or status. However, several studies reveal wealth doesn't equate to happiness. One such study by psychological scientist Cameron Anderson, from the University of California, Berkeley, suggested contentment is related to respect and admiration from those around you and not to money and status. In fact, wealth can cause our behaviour towards other people to worsen! Another study from UC Berkeley found that in San Francisco, where cars must stop at crossings for pedestrians, drivers of luxury cars were four times less likely to give way to pedestrians than those driving less expensive vehicles.

When it comes to mental health, *ubuntu* tells us that unity is our biggest strength. (Solitary confinement in prisons is considered one of the harshest punishments for a reason.) It is ironic that at a time when the digital revolution and social media have brought more interconnectivity into our lives, many people feel more disconnected than ever before and loneliness has reached epidemic proportions. Coming together is vital. But coming together through screens does not make up for good old-fashioned human-to-human interaction.

A study by Brigham Young University in the US has found that loneliness increases the risk of mortality by 26 per cent, and in the UK, over 9 million people – almost a fifth of the population – say they are always or often lonely. In 2018, the prime minister even created a post for a Minister of Loneliness to ensure government policy is put in place to tackle the enormous problem.

THE POWER OF THE MANY

Not only can unity bring us mental well-being but it can also effect powerful change, even against great odds.

In 1930, Mahatma Gandhi rounded up a small group of his supporters to join him on the infamous Salt March. This was a non-violent protest against the British ruling that Indian people were not only to be taxed on salt but also forbidden to collect or sell it, despite it being a staple in cooking. For twenty-four days, Gandhi marched from his ashram in Gujarat to the Arabian Sea to collect salt from the ocean. Hundreds of thousands of people joined him along the way. On his own, Gandhi stood like a single grain of salt, but by the end of the 240 miles the crowd emerged like a rock. The march made Gandhi a popular leader and inspired other peaceful demonstrations that eventually led to India's freedom from colonial rule.

In 1963, civil rights activist Martin Luther King, Jr. appeared in front of a crowd of over 250,000 protesters outside the Lincoln Memorial in Washington, DC. The march was a non-violent protest against racism and inequality, a call for equal rights for African-Americans. When prompted by the crowd, Dr King spoke of his dream of freedom and equality. His 'I have a dream' speech is recognized as one of the greatest in history and was widely seen as a turning point in the fight for civil rights in the United States. Soon afterwards, the US government was forced to listen to the single voice of a unified people that had before been ignored.

In 1989, my grandfather led one of the largest ever anti-apartheid marches. Thirty thousand people marched through the streets of Cape Town. While it was not the first peaceful protest of apartheid, it garnered attention because it came in the middle of a state of emergency when South Africans were not allowed to assemble in large groups, and it inspired other similar marches to take place in Johannesburg and Durban.

STANDING TOGETHER FOR THE COMMON GOOD

Community is defined as 'a group of people living in the same place or having a particular characteristic in common' and 'the condition of sharing or having certain attitudes and interests in common'. *Ubuntu* lies at the heart of the power a crowd can harness for the common good.

You don't have to live in close physical proximity to others in order to experience a sense of community with them. When used for the good, social media can provide an important outlet of expression for many people. Anyone with access to the internet can join in conversations and express themselves and their views across the globe in seconds. We are more connected and able to share information faster than ever before in human history. Millions have posted photos online to show solidarity with cities, such as Paris, which have been hit by terror campaigns.

In 2017, the #MeToo campaign against sexual assault and harassment went viral amid allegations against film producer Harvey Weinstein.

The #BringBackOurGirls campaign highlighted the kidnapping in 2014 of 276 female students from a school in Borno State, Nigeria, by terrorist group Boko Haram.

The #BlackLivesMatter movement began in 2013 as a hashtag and means to bring attention to violence inflicted on black communities following the acquittal of George Zimmerman in the fatal shooting of black teen Trayvon Martin in the US.

Each of the campaigns received massive global attention, partly because so many people shared the hashtag. Sharing a hashtag takes seconds but the reach can be phenomenal.

In times of trauma, human beings seek comfort in togetherness. Perhaps without even knowing the word, we pursue a sense of *ubuntu* as it gives comfort. It encourages us to reach out to our fellow men and women to celebrate all that's good, but also to hold them if they're in pain. Standing shoulder to shoulder with others, physically and spiritually, sends a powerful message. It says, 'I am sad because you are sad. I am suffering because you are suffering.'

Most importantly, it says loud and clear, 'We are one.'

We, the global family, stand united. When we stand against terrorism, we diminish the terror. Unity reminds us there are far more good people in the world than bad.

PEOPLE POWER

In 2014, when an Australian rail commuter slipped and trapped his leg between a Perth-bound train and the platform, scores of passengers joined forces to rescue him. They pushed en masse against the carriage to free the man's leg, which was wedged in the narrow gap. A rescue mission that could have taken hours took a matter of minutes thanks to the help of the man's fellow commuters.

The power of people's shared belief can transform lives not only physically but also spiritually. When twenty-two-year-old Carly Webber from Cornwall fell off a wall, she broke her neck and was left paralysed from the shoulders down. In a split second, her life changed completely. Such a catastrophic disability felt like the end of the world.

Her family supported her, but Carly struggled to see how she could go on. Then, her wider community – members of the village in which she lived – rallied around her to raise money so that she could afford physiotherapy.

Touched by the faith others were showing in her, Carly found an inner strength she never knew she had. Within a year she had regained some movement in her body – something that doctors had previously said would be impossible. Carly defied all the odds because a group of people came together, many of whom were complete strangers, and sent messages of support and offers of help. *Ubuntu* can lift someone up, however hopeless his or her current situation appears.

Even as an individual, you can make a change. You can step in and affect the narrative. By being prepared to put your head above the parapet, you can encourage others to do the same.

On many occasions, my grandfather stepped into crowds to plead for calm during heated protests against apartheid in South Africa. About a year after receiving the Nobel Prize, he found himself near an angry mob in Johannesburg. A car was ablaze. A group of black men jostled to place a tyre around the neck of another black man whom they suspected of collaborating with apartheid forces. They planned to set the tyre alight in a brutal form of punishment known as 'necklacing'. My grandfather physically intervened to stop it from happening. He told everyone that this in-fighting, this lack of unity, undermined the anti-apartheid struggle and, miraculously, they listened.

YOU ARE NOT ALONE

If you think something needs to change because it's unfair or unjust, the likelihood is that others will feel the same way. If we dare to speak up, we will often find we're not a lone voice, but one of many. The world is full of individuals who all want the same thing: a fair and just society, an opportunity to live in peace with good health, a chance to provide for their families, and to feel safe and prosperous. These are fundamental needs of the human condition.

If you believe in something and want to make change happen, the secret is not to give up. Apathy has the power to kill democracy, and erode collective responsibility and the rights of people. If you sign a petition for something you believe in, take a further step and ask yourself: What else can I do? It might be tempting to think, 'That's it. I've done my part.' However, there will always be more you could do, no matter how big or how small.

The MP Jo Cox, who was murdered on a Yorkshire street in June 2016, said, 'We are far more united and have far more in common than that which divides us.' *Ubuntu* teaches us that our force *together* can be a force for good, and there is enormous strength in recognizing the value of our unity, especially if we want to make the world a better place. This is *ubuntu*.

Think of the change you'd like to see in the world. Often people come together when they share a common goal. In an ideal world, what would you like to see happen differently? Whether it's greater peace, or action which helps to protect the environment, or a particular need in your community which you don't think is being met, make a promise to act. Become part of an organization which is doing something to help, or a like-minded group of people. Join a new network. Take up a cause.

How can I find my own community? Not all of us feel we are part of a ready-made community. Many of us live in towns and cities where we hardly know our neighbours. Long working hours and a lack of social activities in the local neighbourhood mean there are few opportunities to meet the people who live near by. A sense of dislocation can be deepened by fractious family relationships, the loss of friendships, working freelance, or having to move home for a new job or partner, but anyone can take steps to rebuild their community.

Here are some ideas:

1. If you're not sure what you're looking for, start with a local group with whom you have something in common. It could be a baby group for new parents, a yoga class or the local five-a-side team, but take the plunge and go along to find your community.

2. Be prepared to show up. Feeling isolated can quickly lead to mental health issues so don't put off until tomorrow what you can do today. There are many different communities out there waiting for you to join them, but it's unlikely they will come knocking at your door. You need to go and find them. It's worth attending more than one meeting to see whether it's the right group for you.

3. Time is the most precious gift you can give. Human bonds are created by offering your time and sharing experiences. Giving your time to someone can be a game-changer. When you meet new people, show interest, listen and ask questions. If it's a new group you're looking for, thousands of charities regularly appeal for people's time. Volunteering for a good cause can help you find like-minded people.

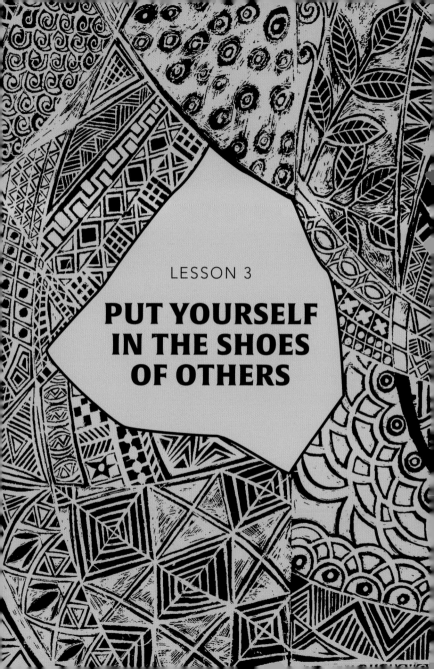

LESSON 3

PUT YOURSELF
IN THE SHOES
OF OTHERS

'If you can learn a simple trick,
Scout, you'll get along a lot better
with all kinds of folks. You never
really understand a person until you
consider things from his point of view,
until you climb inside of his skin and
walk around in it.'

Atticus Finch in Harper Lee's *To Kill a Mockingbird*

Who doesn't like to feel as if they know best or know what's 'right' in a difficult situation? Everyone enjoys the feeling of being the person with all the answers, the person who stands apart from it all and casts judgement.

However, *ubuntu* encourages us to drop our judgements and embrace compassion and understanding. It invites us to turn down the volume of our own (often) self-righteous inner voice and start asking questions on behalf of the other person. Only then can we understand what someone else might be thinking. Or feeling.

EVEN IF YOU DON'T AGREE, CONSIDER THE OTHER SIDE . . .

This was one of many lessons passed down from my grandparents to my mum, and she, in turn, passed it down to me. For my mother, it meant being able to see the position of people living on the other side of one of the most oppressive regimes in the world. It meant trying to understand life from someone else's perspective, even though it was one with which she disagreed passionately.

In Soweto – an abbreviation of South Western Townships – in Johannesburg, she witnessed first hand the oppression of black people. She saw the poor townships where blacks lived, and compared their surroundings to the richer areas populated by whites. She experienced how black children were given an inferior education, little or no access to resources, and denied any of the rights of white kids.

Instead of condemning white people, however, Mum asked herself the question: Would I stand up against apartheid if I were white? She saw the white privilege for what it was – unjust and inhumane – but also understood how easy it must be to accept it as the norm if you'd been socialized constantly to believe in white supremacy. Most people with privilege – racial, social, economic, gender – accept it as a right because it is what they have been taught, and is often the only thing they know.

In the same situation, most of us wouldn't want to give up our privilege or question it, because it simply wouldn't be in our interest to do so. My mum realized that while we might like to think of ourselves as that person who would fight for justice, even in situations where we benefit from injustice, the *majority* of people are not that courageous.

It's human nature to accept the status quo if we gain from it. Maybe some people struggle to know right from wrong or struggle to decide to do the 'right thing'.

This thought gave Mum a different perspective on life and it meant that she didn't see white people as bad necessarily. They became ordinary individuals who enjoyed the fruits of their privilege, and were unwilling to question the source of it and the consequences it had for others.

We learn so many lessons from our parents over the course of our lifetime. Among countless such lessons, my mum taught me not to jump to conclusions. Instead, I should ask questions when someone does something against me, or something that hurts me. According to her, the most important question is always this: In the same circumstances, what would *you* do?

TAKE TIME TO QUESTION

While I was an undergraduate I studied abroad in Sydney and shared a house with a mix of male and female students. One day, a friend from home visited and, during her stay, some of her jewellery went missing. After initial suspicions directed us to one of my female flatmates, feelings of anger and betrayal took over.

How could she do this? I thought we were friends.

It would have been easy to have confronted my flatmate immediately. However, a chat with my mother calmed the heat from my thoughts and my words. She advised me that a direct conversation was necessary, but only once I was calm. I needed to see the other side of the story. We often don't take the time to do this, and in this situation I almost didn't myself.

After a sit-down meeting with all the female housemates, the person I suspected admitted that she had indeed taken the jewellery. That wasn't the end of the story, though. She also confessed that she struggled with an impulse disorder and bulimia. She was fighting a battle nobody was even aware of. She was suffering, and being far from home was exacerbating her internal struggle.

During our chat, my mother had also reminded me of one of my favourite sayings from Ian Maclaren, a Scottish theologian: 'Be kind, for everyone you meet is fighting a hard battle.'

Everyone has difficult things going on in their lives which we know nothing about – even people we think we're close to. Day to day, we might be able to keep our suffering under wraps, but if people around us don't know, they can't help us. We might hide our money or job worries from our families in a bid to protect them, or might keep problems secret from friends because we don't want to appear to be moaning all the time. However, this also keeps the gift of *ubuntu* from helping us too.

By being kind and by treading carefully, my friend and I avoided further harming someone who was already suffering.

TALK TO PEOPLE

Walking in another person's shoes is the ability to see things from their perspective. It isn't easy. What if you have nothing in common with them? Or you've been hurt badly by their actions? Just the idea of *trying* to see the other side of the story can be a challenge. But what we can gain from trying is always more than we could ever imagine. My grandfather once said, 'If you want peace you don't talk to your friends, you talk to your enemies.'

Talking to those with opposing views is exactly what the Tutu Foundation in the UK encouraged people to do when it was launched in 2007. One programme called Conversations for Change encouraged community groups experiencing difficulties to speak to one another. The focus was on creating a dialogue between parties that were in the same geographic community but in differing social ones, and bringing together the two opposing sides.

The values of the Foundation are based on *ubuntu*, as its mission is to build peace, respect, understanding and connections between people. The Ubuntu Youth Project has been particularly successful and, over the years, has helped improve relationships between police and disaffected youths.

Many remarkable things have happened at the table, which we called the Ubuntu Round Table, and behind the scenes. For the first time, many teenagers have been introduced to the meaning of *ubuntu*. In workshops, they've been given the space to discuss the ideas behind the philosophy and have been encouraged to consider another individual's point of view. Perhaps also for the first time.

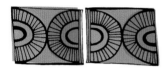

CONSIDER WHAT SOMEONE ELSE MIGHT BE THINKING

A teenager who had signed up for one of the programmes turned up one morning with a big plaster on his neck. When the youth worker asked him what had happened, he explained that he'd been stabbed by another teen on the estate where he lived. It was an unprovoked attack and he'd needed stitches. Expecting him to be angry and out for revenge, the youth worker asked the boy how he was feeling.

'Yes, I'm OK,' he replied. 'I'm hurt, but I've decided not to hold a grudge because I have no idea what the guy who did this was going through that day. He could be facing all kinds of things I know nothing about, and maybe he just lost it that morning.'

You are not alone if his response makes your jaw drop. This teenager knew it wasn't a personal attack and understood full well how tough life could be on his estate. He made the choice to walk in the other person's shoes. This is *ubuntu.*

Putting yourself in the shoes of others is a conscious choice. If you can't understand someone's words or actions, try to imagine what might be happening in their life. What's caused them to behave in this way? Where do they live? Who do they live with? What are their life circumstances? Ask yourself if their actions might be a reflection of someone who is content or someone who is struggling to live their life.

Most of what people do when they hurt others is *not* personal. Often they are reacting to their upbringing, events or experiences from their childhood that happened years ago. By spending a few moments considering why and how they made their choices, we can start to feel very differently about our so-called enemies.

I once saw a quote in passing that read: 'Four plus eight equals twelve, but so does six plus six.' Someone's perspective might be different to yours, but it doesn't mean theirs is wrong. We can all reach the same conclusion differently, or different conclusions (and no better and no worse!) because we are not the same.

FIND INSPIRATION IN OTHERS' JOURNEYS

In April 1994, my grandfather finally got to vote for the first time in the first free and fair elections in South Africa following the collapse of apartheid. He was sixty-three. Once he had seen Nelson Mandela sweep into power, my grandfather planned to take a well-earned retirement, but life had other plans for him. He was selected to chair the Truth and Reconciliation Commission (TRC), which essentially administered court-like restorative justice and seen as the best way to move the country forward to begin to heal the wounds of apartheid.

The leaders of the new South Africa could have followed the example of the Nuremberg Trials, which took place after the Second World War. They had seen how, with Nuremberg and other trials, imprisonment and death sentences most often simply start a new cycle of victimization, with calls for retaliation and vengeance. These trials showcased to the world those who were guilty of crimes against humanity in Nazi Germany. The perpetrators were tried and sentenced to terms in prison – and even to death – for their role in the atrocities that occurred in Germany and in the countries it fought and annexed.

Many people in South Africa said that, given the extent of the country's apartheid atrocities, Nuremberg-style trials were indeed the only way to go. However, true to their African culture, South Africa's leaders decided that, through the TRC, they had an opportunity to show the world a different way of rebuilding a nation post conflict.

The idea was that all parties in South Africa would be allowed to relate their experiences so that South Africans could hear the whole story of apartheid. It was necessary for the country as a whole to bear witness to the extent of the atrocities carried out both in upholding apartheid and in the attempts to overthrow it. It was a groundbreaking attempt to drain the wound and heal South Africa.

My grandfather supported the idea wholly. He thought that if people were to become 'one' again, they needed to share a common history. And you can only do that if you are allowed to experience what the other side has experienced. This includes listening to their thoughts, understanding their beliefs and ideas, and even empathizing with their motivations. Perpetrators of crimes in South Africa during apartheid were invited to provide testimony with full disclosure, and the TRC was permitted to grant them amnesty if the crimes were held to be politically motivated. Every single painful case was broadcast on television.

One of those heard was that of Amy Biehl, a white American Fulbright scholar who had supported the anti-apartheid movement. One day in August 1993, Amy was pulled from her car. She was stabbed and stoned to death by a mob. Four black men were convicted of her murder and sent to jail. Then, during the TRC, they were pardoned when it was determined that their actions had been politically motivated.

Biehl's family supported this decision. For a parent to forgive the murder of their child is unthinkable for many, but the Biehls were able to take their forgiveness a huge step further. They met the families of the murderers, built a community organization with them and invested economically in the community from which the young men had come.

How did they do this? The Biehls made a choice to walk in the shoes of their daughter's killers. They listened to stories about their poor, violent upbringing. They heard how they had been returning from a political rally when they spotted Amy driving her three black friends in a car. For them, Amy symbolized the white oppressor. She was not an individual. Black people had been treated as second-class citizens for so long, it had become possible for these men to dehumanize other people, just as they had been dehumanized themselves.

This deep understanding of circumstances allowed Amy's parents to forgive and then to move on to create the Amy Biehl Foundation, a not-for-profit organization against violence. In 2015, when Amy's mother, Linda Biehl, took part in a discussion about restorative justice at Whittier College in the US with one of her daughter's killers, she said that she now *understood* how the killers were not responsible for Amy's death.

The Truth and Reconciliation Commission encouraged people to forgive, but forgiveness was never forced on them. It *couldn't* be forced on them. It only works when someone chooses to walk in someone else's shoes.

If you're in conflict with someone in your life, try doing the same. *Ubuntu* tells us that compassion and empathy for the other side will only serve us well. We might even find we'd react the same way as others have done, if we were to wear their shoes for the day.

Shoe-shifting – really imagining putting on those other shoes. If you find yourself in conflict with someone or passing judgement, take a moment to engage with his or her side of the story. Close your eyes and imagine how they might be feeling about the situation. What chain of events led them to their own beliefs, however misguided, and their reactions, however damaging? How might they jump to conclusions? Can you imagine reacting as they have done? Even attempting to do this is a powerful exercise.

Consider the shoes *you* are wearing. Try to stop thinking, 'But I'm right about this!' Even if you feel completely justified in your beliefs and that there's no room for doubt – because there's always room for growth. In the Alcoholics Anonymous Twelve-Step programme, step ten recommends that participants do a 'daily review' to increase their responsibility and encourage them to see things from others' perspectives. Doing this can bring tranquillity to our lives. Resentment breeds inner turmoil.

This step can encourage you to:

1. Look at a situation honestly, including viewing it from the other side;

2. Admit when you're wrong and forgive where appropriate;

3. Ask yourself some difficult questions and be prepared to answer honestly. Are you feeling so angry about a situation that it's clouding your judgement? Does it feel overly important that you are viewed as 'right', and why is this? If you accept that someone else's perspective is different to your own, does this make you feel differently about your own opinion?

Say the other person's point of view out loud. As a child, whenever I argued with my brother, my mother would suggest I tell her – in my own words – what he was trying to say. Verbalizing the other side of the argument is a powerful practice. Often, it's easy to miss the point someone else is trying to make, because you're so wrapped up in your own narrative. Try speaking aloud the other person's perspective, as if you're trying to persuade a third person to see their side of the story. It's a humbling exercise.

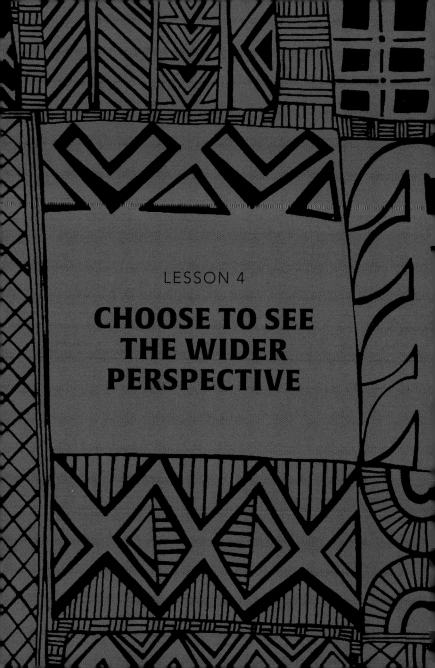

LESSON 4

CHOOSE TO SEE
THE WIDER
PERSPECTIVE

'If you want to know the end,
look at the beginning.'

African proverb

'When the music changes so
does the dance.'

African proverb

Even more than trying to walk in someone else's shoes, choosing to see the wider perspective on life can be a challenge – the idea goes beyond appreciating life from another person's point of view. *Ubuntu* teaches us that we should actively look at the world from *every* perspective, from *every* angle. By doing this we can gain as much understanding as possible about a situation.

Imagine that you're an astronaut. You've finally reached your destination in space and, in a quiet moment, have a few minutes to peer down to planet Earth. Unsurprisingly, seeing the reality of our fragile sphere, hanging like a blue marble in the empty void, can be a life-changing experience. The borders of countries, the wars, the conflicts, the environmental challenges all pale into insignificance because you're seeing our planet as a whole. It's unfathomably small and alone.

From this perspective, many astronauts describe an overwhelming urge to protect our planet and, for perhaps the first time, experience an intense appreciation of the sanctity of life. Because life *is* fragile, and so is the planet on which we're living. We forget this when we're caught up in everyday life with the pressures of education, work, family, and the general busyness of our modern existence. This startling effect on an astronaut's life has even been given its own name. It's known as the 'overview effect'.

Just like a space explorer, we earthlings can decide to look for the 'overview', the bigger picture, of any situation too. The only time we can't change a perspective is if we refuse to try, or have an unreasonable attachment to a particular outcome. Seeing the wider perspective allows us to pay attention to the stories that determine what it is we and those on the other side see. If you're committed to believing only one version of events, and resolutely insist on viewing a situation from one perspective, it's unlikely you'll be able to make the subtle shifts necessary either to make progress in getting what you want or to feel any compassion for those for whom the other side of the story is true.

We are not expected to try to make lies out to be the truth, but we are called to know for ourselves the roots of those lies. It is only in allowing ourselves to take a 360-degree view of any given situation that we are actually able to make just and compassionate decisions and actions. The ability to see the wider perspective is what allows great leaders such as Mandela to come to the table with their enemies and recognize that those against whom they struggle also have a story to share. This ability is also what allowed him to make those subtle shifts necessary to make progress in getting what he wanted and to feel compassion for those on the other side.

EVERY PERSON'S PERSPECTIVE MATTERS

Viewing the atrocities committed during apartheid from the other perspective – a wider perspective – was what the Truth and Reconciliation Commission set out to achieve. It was designed to have oversight of the whole, prolonged conflict from the perspectives of black and white, rich and poor, male and female, and to leave no stone unturned that might help to throw up some answers.

The TRC hearings were held all over South Africa, from the smallest towns to the biggest cities. The Commission would often take a week to listen to the testimonies of those involved, so everyone who needed to could tell their stories. A simultaneous translation service was arranged so that people could testify in their home language. Special hearings to accommodate many perspectives were organized for different institutions, including the medical profession, business leaders and religious communities.

The idea was this: the perspective of *everyone* was welcomed. Even those imprisoned for their crimes. If the wider perspective could be understood through as many eyes as possible, then perhaps moving on would be possible too.

The world watched in awe as South Africa put *ubuntu* into action, purging its wounds live on radio and television, and then granting amnesty to those who had taken part in crimes if they could prove they had acted for political reasons. It was a painful and painstaking process but one that was designed to help heal divisions. It was for the greater good. Those who had been wronged were encouraged to forgive, not only for their own well-being but also for the benefit of the nation. Those responsible for the TRC saw this as the only way forward towards building national unity, this acknowledgement of all who considered South Africa their home.

'May your choices reflect your hopes, not your fears.'

Nelson Mandela

Choosing to view the bigger picture – and it's important to realize that it *is* a choice – can help us feel compassion for the point of view of others. It can help us to understand why something has happened and to deal with it more sensitively. It can turn anger into understanding and hatred into compassion. By widening our horizons we can grow as a person, rather than remaining stuck in our own world view. We feel better about ourselves. If we remain fixated on self-righteousness we can end up bitter and living in a divided community incapable of finding common ground.

Ubuntu teaches us that change is possible *however* bad the situation. If we look around us and ask questions of our fellow people we can find answers there. Answers that might astound us.

THE WORSE THE SITUATION, THE WIDER THE PERSPECTIVE NEEDS TO BE

In 1994, over a period of just one hundred days, many Hutu people in Rwanda slaughtered thousands of Tutsi people, a community who were in the minority but who had long dominated the country. The Hutus killed an estimated 800,000 Tutsis, roughly 70 per cent of the Tutsi population. Neighbours killed neighbours. Some Hutu husbands killed their Tutsi wives.

Christophe Mbonyingabo was exiled after his family fled their home country. He lost his father and brothers in the violence. He became embittered and full of hatred. Once the war was over, he returned to Rwanda but felt as though he had nothing. No family. No home. Nothing to live for.

In despair, he went to a church where he listened to a preacher talk about the divisions between the two communities. He heard how the other side was suffering too, as Hutus had left the country in droves during the last days of the genocide. They had fled because, once a Tutsi rebel group had overthrown the Hutu-controlled government, moderate Hutus began to be killed by Hutu extremists and Tutsis alike in 'revenge killings'.

For the first time, Christophe appreciated that each ethnic group was suffering in its own way. Nobody had escaped the pain. It belonged to the Hutus as much as it belonged to the Tutsis. He began to consider the terrible events from many different angles, and thought about all the hatred and turmoil those hundred days had brought. None of it had been positive for anyone involved, he reasoned. At a time when anyone's belief in God would be challenged, Christophe discovered that his faith could help break down the barriers. This was his answer.

When Christophe returned to live in Rwanda, working alongside Christian relief charity Tearfund, he eventually helped to set up a group whose mission it was to bring survivors and offenders together. Able to see the war from both sides, Christophe shared his new, wider perspective and encouraged others to do the same.

Through his work, one day he met villagers who lived side by side but still hadn't reconciled years after the conflict. One survivor hadn't greeted or spoken to a neighbour for twenty-two years, but with Christophe's gentle help they managed to find forgiveness, leaving their bitterness and hatred behind.

Christophe also developed Peace Clubs in high schools, where children are taught exactly how and why the massacre happened. The idea is that if the next generation sees the wider perspective and understands how and why genocide has occurred in the past, then they are less inclined to cause future wars and mass killings. It's less likely that history will repeat itself.

CHANGING YOUR OWN PERSPECTIVE *IS* POSSIBLE

It's all too easy to remain stuck in our views and opinions of the world, but there is freedom to be found when we choose to look for the wider perspective.

Many people have preconceived ideas about individuals living on the streets. One 2018 UK study, as part of a survey by the Museum of Homelessness, shows how neuroscience can even explain how our brains actually dehumanize others, something called 'the bystander effect'.

'If you don't like something, change it. If you can't change it, change your attitude.'

Maya Angelou

Participants admitted that when they think of people experiencing homelessness, they think of 'criminality' and 'despair', and that it's 'their problem' and they are 'there for a reason'. Failing to feel compassion can be a common reaction towards individuals who find themselves in this situation.

The compassionate approach is one that is being nurtured through work done by the Tutu Foundation in the UK. We've recently joined forces with the British Transport Police to help officers understand the possible life experiences of those they encounter in their everyday work. It's all too easy to jump to conclusions about someone's situation, but we're helping to train officers to ask relevant questions that will help get to the heart of a situation.

I was told the story of one BTP officer who had not received the training yet, but who employed the compassionate approach that the Foundation planned to teach him and his colleagues. He came across a young woman who hadn't paid her train fare. Instead of taking the woman's details and handing her the statutory fine, the officer trusted his gut instinct and chose to ask her some questions about her circumstances instead.

Surprised by the officer's genuine concern, the young woman opened up to him. She admitted she had jumped on the train to escape terrible domestic violence. She poured out her story. She was trying to get away from her situation but didn't have enough money for a ticket. The officer, moved by her plight, ended up staying with her for hours until he could figure out how to help her and direct her to the appropriate services.

The Tutu Foundation is an advocate of asking 'why' someone has made the choices they have rather than leaping to conclusions. Behind the question of 'why' is the chance to see a wider perspective.

Ubuntu teaches us that not everyone will share this view, however. We are all products of our culture and values, our upbringing and our life experience, our own particular set of character traits. And we naturally make sense of the world according to these factors. As a result, our version of reality often isn't the same as someone else's. The only way of breaking out of this cycle of tunnel vision is to ask questions, in a compassionate way, of people we don't agree with or even necessarily feel we want to understand. What seems reasonable to them might seem ridiculous to us. However, if we can step outside our own perspective, we might discover that our view is not as valid as we thought.

A study by Stanford psychologist Carol Dweck in the 1970s showed that there are two different types of mind-set.

The 'fixed mind-set', where a person believes their basic qualities – their talents or intelligence – are fixed traits. Or a 'growth mind-set', where a person's qualities can change with hard work, experience or self-belief. Through her studies with school children, Dweck proved that if you are instilled with a love of learning and taught how to build resilience you can develop your accomplishments and understanding – at any age.

Decades later, Dweck's work still illustrates that every human being is capable of changing their viewpoint and opening their minds to greater understanding. We need to be mindful about choosing to see other people's perspectives. We also need to see the wider perspective in our own lives.

Looking from a distance makes it easier to see the bigger picture. If you're struggling to get some perspective on a situation, take a step back. Ask for another person's viewpoint: 'What would you do differently to what I'm doing now?' Ask yourself: 'Will this problem matter to me in a week? A month? A year?' This will give you an idea of its importance and the real impact it might have on your life.

'This too shall pass' is a comforting saying in challenging situations. Nothing is static, change is inevitable. Sometimes we have to allow time for this to happen.

If you're struggling to appreciate someone else's reaction or perspective, think about what led them to this place – often it may not be about you, but about something in their own personal story.

Focus on what life has given you, rather than denied you. At a 6 a.m. boxing class, my instructor once yelled, 'We all want to complain about having to get up to do a 6 a.m. workout. But let's be thankful we actually *can* get up to do a 6 a.m. workout!' This startled me, but she was absolutely right. We should be grateful for what we *can* do rather than focusing on what we cannot.

Practise gratitude. It's a sure-fire way to quickly shift your perspective in an intense moment to something wider and therefore calmer. If you're feeling stuck, look beyond the immediate issue and write down five things you could do right now that are within your control.

Try new things. Sounds simple? It is. Shaking up things a little can have a profound effect on us. More experiences and knowledge naturally give us a wider perspective on life. Try something from an unfamiliar culture: a recipe from a different continent for a meal you've never tried before; a local Polish or Chinese shop you've often walked past but not ventured into. Read a book or watch a film from a genre you've never attempted. Even if you don't like the new experience you might still learn something from it. On the other hand, you might find out it's something you never knew you liked.

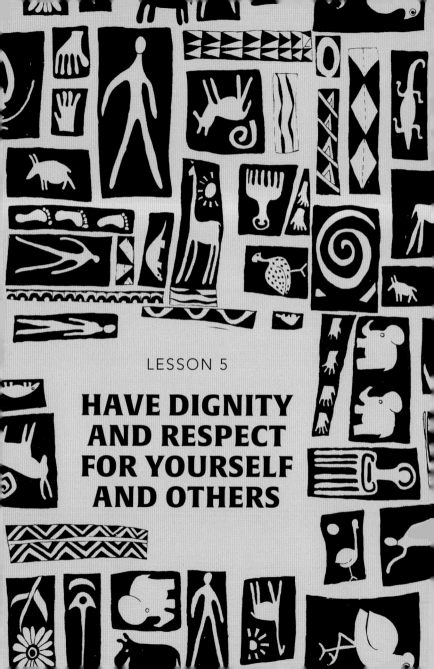

LESSON 5

HAVE DIGNITY
AND RESPECT
FOR YOURSELF
AND OTHERS

'"African people did not hear of culture for the first time from Europeans; their societies were not mindless, but frequently had a philosophy of great depth and value and beauty; they had poetry, and above all, they had dignity."'

Chinua Achebe in Jayalakshmi V. Rao, *Proverb and Culture in the Novels of Chinua Achebe*

Perhaps the most crucial underlying principle of *ubuntu* is respect, both for oneself and for other people. It's a simple idea. If a person respects himself or herself, they are far more likely to extend that to other people.

Let's go back to my grandfather's words: 'We believe that a person is a person through other persons, that my humanity is caught up, is inextricably bound up, in yours. When I dehumanize you, I inexorably dehumanize myself.' By this logic, respect must begin from within.

However, isn't 'looking after oneself' – the idea of self-care – a selfish act? Is it the same as 'looking after number one', meaning that we are putting ourselves first, above all others?

Ubuntu has taught me this isn't so. *Ubuntu* means believing in other people, regardless of who they are and what their role is in life. Everyone is the same and deserving of our respect. We don't pick and choose the people to whom we show it. However, *ubuntu* also means believing in ourselves and showing ourselves respect too.

If we're going to decide to live with *ubuntu* in our lives, we must look after ourselves. We have to give ourselves what we need on both a physical and mental level in order for our bodies and minds not only to attend to our daily business but also to have room for others.

This might mean that you need regular time to yourself to take stock and reflect; to be mindful and sit quietly. Or perhaps to eat healthily or take daily exercise. Whatever self-care means to you, do it!

YOU CAN'T POUR FROM AN EMPTY CUP

Before an aeroplane takes off, the flight attendants always deliver advice on what to do in an emergency situation. They explain that if the oxygen masks drop down, because of a fall in oxygen levels at high altitude, passengers should always attach their own masks before trying to help others – including their own children – put on theirs. After all, if you pass out from lack of oxygen, what good are you to anyone else? And this applies to all aspects of life.

My mother learned this lesson the hard way. She brought up me and my brother, Mpilo, as a single mother, while working and being a committed activist for peace and race and gender equality. She is one of the most selfless people I know but rarely takes time out, and this lifestyle can leave her exhausted.

One evening in the early 2000s, her approach to the overbearing demands of a busy life changed. She was due to give a speech alongside the Northern Irish Nobel Peace Prize winner Betty Williams at a university, but everyone was running late. Their flights had been delayed and both Betty and my mother were being rushed from the airport to the hotel. They were then expected to be downstairs, ready to go on stage, as quickly as possible.

My mother was given thirty minutes to prepare herself.

She set about racing around, changing her clothes and freshening up, and by the time she had run down to the lobby to announce herself, Betty had only just arrived. The organizers told Betty to hurry too, but she smiled and politely declined. She told them clearly and calmly that there was always time. She needed to collect herself, have a cup of tea – maybe a glass of wine. Very nicely she explained that she needed to feel fully rested to perform well and to give the best possible presentation. It was in everyone's best interests.

My mother was impressed and remembers thinking, 'Wow! People are able to say this and it's OK?' This had not been how she had lived her life up until this point. However, she saw that Betty had come up with a solution that worked for her as well as for others, without putting herself last – an outlook which embodies the spirit of *ubuntu*. Respectful boundaries are needed so that we can look after ourselves and continue to give to others.

After all, nobody can be expected to pour from an empty cup.

This idea of self-respect being intertwined with respect for others is relevant on a larger scale as well as a personal one.

According to the World Health Organization, hunger is one of the biggest threats to human life on this planet, and adequate nutrition has always been a challenge facing the populations of many African countries.

A group of villages in Lesotho embodies *ubuntu* as it helps to feed the women living there, who then have the strength to spend their energy on feeding the village children – a thousand of them so far. A charity called Msizi

Africa, set up by Lucy Herron in 2007, provides the food in this desperately poor part of the country. It believes that in order for children to grow up healthy and strong, and to reach their full potential, they need a nourishing meal every day as good nutrition is critical for development. The charity provides the women of the village with rice, chicken and fish, and leaves to them the preparation and serving. So far the women have served over 2.8 million meals this way.

This is just one example of lots of charitable work in which communities are helped to help themselves through education, feeding programmes and seed funding for businesses. It's *ubuntu* in action.

DON'T BE AFRAID TO ASK FOR HELP

Seeking help doesn't come naturally to many of us. *Ubuntu* means recognizing other people in yourself, yet turning to other people for assistance can sometimes feel like the hardest thing in the world to do. We worry that it might be viewed as a sign of weakness. It can feel embarrassing – revealing that we don't know enough or don't have the ability to do something. We fear feeling stupid or being seen as unable to cope. And we don't know for sure how the person we're turning to will respond. Pride or low self-esteem can lead us to pretend nothing is wrong.

Our world – or at least the Western world – is obsessed with the idea of individualism, the belief that personal needs are more important than the needs of society as a whole. A joint study by the Universities of Waterloo and Arizona State, covering a fifty-year period, examined factors linked with individualism, such as family size, higher divorce rates and job trends. Led by behavioural scientists Igor Grossmann and Henri C. Santos, it found individualism first developed in the baby-boomer generation, and evolved alongside an increase in wealth and education in the United States.

The well-known phrase 'pull oneself up by one's bootstraps' underscores the messages of individualism in our culture and leads us to believe we should provide for ourselves, so people end up suffering because they don't feel as if they can ask for help. At best we might turn to a self-help book or browse the internet for answers to our problems. Why do we find it so hard to turn to other people?

When I was at boarding school, the teachers encouraged students to ask for help, especially as we reached our teenage years, when life starts to get complicated. They told us, 'We can only help if we know you're struggling.'

Before people can help you, they have to see your need.

This invitation made it much easier for us students to speak up when things weren't going well. It's not always that easy to know that help is at hand, though. Many of us fear being rejected. When you're feeling vulnerable and struggling, the last thing you want to hear is, 'No, I can't help you.'

Take heart, however. The reality is that many people like to help others. When a friend turns to you for advice, you likely feel flattered and want to do a good turn, don't you? Helping others makes a person feel wanted, needed and good about themselves. So reach out and have a little faith.

THESE PEOPLE ARE TRULY PEOPLE

Dignity is empowering and enables us to recognize one another's humanity. If someone acts in a dignified manner, it can have a bearing on the way they will be treated by others.

Respect goes hand in hand with dignity. My mother once told me the story of a butcher's shop in the community in which she grew up in Soweto. On the face of things it was an ordinary shop, selling everything from chicken drumsticks to pork chops. What made it special, however, were the people who worked there. Every single person who walked in the door – young or old, black or white, rich or poor – received exactly the same welcome.

While other shopkeepers in the community ignored young kids and served adults first, this particular one treated everyone equally. They smiled, looked each customer in the eye and, with sincerity, asked them how their day was. Even if the person in front of the counter was knee-high, they were afforded the same respect as an elder. This was highly unusual at the time, but kids quickly picked up on how they were being treated as they ran errands for their parents.

People began to hear about the quality of customer care at this butcher's and started to come to visit and experience it for themselves. They came to spend their precious money there, in the shop where *ubuntu* was part of the service. Customers would say, 'These people are truly people,' as the owner and his staff embodied the philosophy of *ubuntu* in each and every human interaction.

When people have the gift of *ubuntu* they maintain this standard even on bad days, or in the most mundane situations. They respect themselves. They respect others.

LOOK BEYOND THE LABEL

When we afford dignity and respect to others we should try to avoid labels at all costs as they reinforce prejudices. Labels pigeonhole us and subdivide us into categories, which can be difficult or impossible to shake off. A person is more than what society 'says' they are.

Recently, in the United States, the phrase 'a person who is experiencing homelessness' has become more common, rather than 'a homeless person'. Anyone experiencing homelessness is first and foremost a person. They are not defined by their situation. Their homelessness may be long term or short term, but it is not all there is to know about them.

Stigma is also often attached to labels. Survivors of rape or domestic abuse, for example, often feel shamed by their experience, and there is still prejudice in different regions of the world towards people living with AIDS.

When describing someone, be mindful of the label you are placing upon him or her – consciously or unconsciously – and what it might mean to them and therefore to you. Look beyond what you might first see.

Dignity gives us space to be ourselves. It means we feel valued in the world – valued for what we believe in, for our work in or out of the home, and for our place in society.

Often it's a vocation, passion or mission that affords us this privilege. A passion or a vocation is a blessing but whatever it is we do, believing in it, doing it with pride and to the best of our ability fosters that sense of dignity.

Over the years I have had dealings with Virgin, a company run by my grandfather's friend, businessman Sir Richard Branson. At Virgin they have a philosophy when it comes to their workforce: 'Train people well enough so they can leave, treat them well enough so they don't want to.' Their ethos is to afford staff enough dignity that they feel well treated, and as a result will be more productive. And it works. Virgin Unite gives employees the freedom to work remotely where they want – you could spend a week in Berlin or Ibiza. These employees continue to deliver excellent work wherever they are in the world because they have the expertise needed to do their job and the trust of their employer.

THE PEACE DIGNITY CAN BRING

Sometimes the essence of *ubuntu* and the dignity it brings can be found in the most unexpected places. When we adopt the spirit of *ubuntu* anything is possible.

Following the Ebola crisis of 2014 in Sierra Leone, families were not allowed to bury their dead. The authorities were worried about contagion and spreading the disease further. However, leaving the dead unburied or piled into mass graves went against cultural beliefs. It also made the pain of losing loved ones even harder to bear. This led to families hiding the bodies of their relatives or trying to inter them in unsuitable ground. Eventually, charities such as CAFOD stepped in to help organize burial teams, so families could lay their loved ones to rest with dignity.

The need for dignity also extended as far as bringing together religious leaders. Priests worked alongside imams to organize proper funerals for the victims of the disease. The suffering of the families came first, and their grief was afforded the space and dignity it deserved.

Dignity in death became a big issue for my family when my grandfather's prostate cancer returned and he fell seriously ill. He wasn't expected to survive long. He thought the end was nigh and was very vocal about his beliefs in maintaining his dignity if he were to face his dying day.

For him, there is no self-respect left if you are suffering unbearably and coming to the end of your life, yet provided with no choice but to continue suffering. Thankfully, it wasn't my grandfather's time then and although the cancer is recurring, he continues to fight his illness. However, in 2016, on his eighty-fifth birthday he wrote an article about his wish to have the option of assisted death when his time does come. Two years previously he had also written in the *Guardian* that, 'Just as I have argued firmly for compassion and fairness in life, I believe terminally ill people should be treated with the same compassion and fairness when it comes to their deaths.'

Dignity gives us peace. If a loved one dies in dignified circumstances we can feel comforted, despite our grief, knowing they might have suffered less.

Whatever is happening in your life, giving yourself and others dignity and respect provides comfort and empowerment. It can make you feel better in uncertain times and help you to see the bigger picture – that when people have their dignity they feel empowered, and empowered people empower more people in turn. It's what we all deserve.

When 'help me' feels an impossible ask, think about this:

1. **Most people love helping others.** It's flattering to be asked for help, and by reaching out for assistance everyone feels less alone, because we all – whoever we are – face problems in our lives. Challenges and upsets exist for every living, breathing human being, often on a daily basis. Sharing our struggles is part of our humanity.

2. **Step outside yourself.** If you find it hard to ask someone else to be your friend, try to be your own friend. Write down your problem and then imagine someone else asking you for help to solve it. What would you say to them? You could also find an organization or charity that might assist you. Online forums can be very useful too, as they can give us help anonymously if we feel unable to speak out loud about any difficulties we might be facing.

3. **Know you are not alone.** Unless you have arrived from another planet there isn't a single other human being who has not encountered a problem similar to yours. Help will be out there.

What do you need to bring dignity into your day?
Each day, most of us need to eat wholesome food, take exercise of some kind (even if it's just a walk), feel a sense of community by talking with others, and have a purpose in order to feel at our best. If we aren't able to meet our basic needs, it's harder to afford ourselves respect and dignity.

Recognize what makes you feel better or worse. When unhappiness sets in, and you feel dissatisfied with life, it's often accompanied by a sense of restlessness. You can end up reaching outside yourself for distraction of any kind, often fuelling unhealthy habits. In the hope of cheering yourself, you might find yourself shopping for things you can't really afford, looking up a former partner online – someone you should steer clear of – or scrolling mindlessly through social media. All to fill a gap. Recognizing these moments and taking stock of your behaviour and motives before you do something that will make you feel worse is key. Whether it's deleting social media apps on your phone or going for a long walk in nature, often taking ourselves out of the situation can provide immediate relief.

***Your* opinion of *you* is what matters most.** A phrase often attributed to former first lady of the United States Eleanor Roosevelt is, 'No one can make you feel inferior

without your consent.' It's a quote you can find displayed on the walls of schools, for example, intended to inspire young minds. If you suffer from low self-esteem, though, it's very tough to have a high opinion of yourself – it's difficult not to feel inferior.

Our internal voice then often mirrors our experiences in life. If your everyday outlook is negative and you approach life expecting the worst, it's far more likely that others will respond negatively to you, and your life experience will become a negative one. It then becomes a vicious circle. By contrast, if you like yourself, you are more likely to see the good in others and they'll see the good in you. We were all born with a purpose before people were able to form opinions of us. Take care of yourself. Focus on your positives. Learn a new skill. Connect with people who love you.[1]

[1] www.mind.org

To escape the negative cycle of self-criticism:

1. **Recognize you're caught in a cycle.** Whether we are criticizing our appearance every time we look in a mirror ('I'm so fat/I hate my double chin/I hate my wonky teeth'), our role in life ('My job is so low paid/I'm bored staying at home with the kids/I'm a low achiever') or our self-esteem ('Nobody likes me/I hate being anxious'), we can talk negatively to ourselves without realizing it, and it can dominate our internal monologue. This destructive self-talk creates an image of ourselves that's hard to break unless we recognize we're doing it in the first place.

2. **View your negative self-image as a flame.** The more you fan the flame (by criticizing yourself), the more the fire burns. It's time to dampen it with positive talk. Look in the mirror and decide on something you *do* like about yourself. Think of the lovely things your friends have said about you in the past, or think of a successful moment from your life. Small steps lead to bigger ones.

3. **You have the power to break the cycle.** Spot your triggers. Do you feel worse at certain times of the day (in the morning rush or when you're tired in the evening)? If so, change your routine. Note down positive affirmations (my personal favourite is 'what is coming is better than what has gone') and stick them around your mirror to read as you get ready in the morning, write in a gratitude journal every evening before bed, walk to work along a different route for a change of scenery, or go somewhere different on your lunch break. Even avoiding people who drain your energy is acceptable if you want to break your cycle. Simply being mindful of how your reality is distorted by negativity can be the start of change!

4. **Be kind to yourself.** Whenever I used to feel bad about myself or spoke about myself in a negative manner, my mother would tell me to be nice to her daughter because she thought her daughter was pretty great. Now, when a friend talks about herself to me in a poor way, I ask her to please be nice to my friend because I think very highly of her. Step outside yourself and see the good.

LESSON 6

BELIEVE IN
THE GOOD OF
EVERYONE

'I believe each one of us is a saint until the contrary is proven.'

Archbishop Desmond Tutu

'People are human beings, produced by the society in which they live. You encourage people by seeing the good in them.'

Nelson Mandela

Every day, when we switch on the news, scroll through social media or browse a newspaper, we hear about the terrible things of which people are capable. Our minds become saturated with stories of murder, rape, war, hunger, poverty and crisis.

Terrible things do happen and they make the world a challenging place. A *far greater* number of good deeds are performed by people, however, but these are rarely reported. Every day, everywhere, a million small (and sometimes big!) acts of love, devotion, selflessness and unity are carried out, which encapsulate and celebrate our humanity. It's just that good news and small acts of kindness don't make good headlines.

My mother and grandfather have always been big believers in the inherent goodness of people. They *choose* to look for the basic good in humanity and you're far more likely to find it if you too choose to look for it.

WHATEVER THE CIRCUMSTANCES, GOOD CAN PREVAIL

A few summers ago, I had the opportunity to travel to Palestine to meet some Palestinian people and to stay with a family there. Fascinated by the Middle East and saddened by its ongoing conflicts, I took up the chance to go with a group comprising mostly Americans, along with a few British and South African travellers, to learn about this troubled land. The humanity I discovered in such a divided place humbled me.

Five of us stayed with a woman called Salah and her family. She was the perfect host who welcomed us with open arms. It would have been easy to imagine she'd had a carefree life by the way she behaved, but over tea and sweets, in a gentle voice, she told us the story of what had happened to her family.

Shortly after Salah gave birth to her first son, her husband was imprisoned for giving food to someone in need who the authorities mistakenly believed was involved in terrorism. Over the years, three of her four sons had been arrested. They were all released eventually, though not without a legal battle and with help from the organizers of our trip in the case of one of her sons.

This story was typical for Palestinians, who can be imprisoned for all kinds of misdemeanours – from posting something on Facebook deemed inappropriate to providing food to neighbours suspected of wrongdoing.

What struck me, once Salah had finished speaking, was the light and kindness in her eyes. The basic goodness inside her hadn't been diminished by her terrible experiences. She looked for the good in us, too. She still cared for others deeply, even allowing Americans – the people of a nation often seen to ignore or exacerbate Palestinian oppression – into her home. She still wanted to feed and look after us all, sharing the little she had.

Seeking out the good in others often starts by finding a simple connection with their humanity. One way of doing this is by looking for common ground. It might feel like a struggle, especially if you have different opinions or if you have other reasons to dislike them.

'When you choose to see the good in others, you end up finding the good in yourself.'

Anonymous

Our world leaders and politicians are tasked with the difficult objective of mediating peace in volatile countries, from Syria to Northern Ireland. Meeting meaningfully with someone with whom you've been in conflict, or who holds opposing beliefs, has to be one of the most challenging positions in which a human can find themself. You might have good reason to think you have nothing in common.

Lord Peter Hain, an ambassador for the Tutu Foundation, learned to foster relationships of trust during his involvement with Ireland's peace process talks, even when divisions ran deep. He understood trust is the most important foundation of human relationships and it needs to be built or restored – either inside or outside a professional setting – if we are to work effectively with people.

For Lord Hain the secret always lay in trying to uncover the point of human contact beyond the 'tension of politics'. One day he found himself chatting to the then Sinn Féin leader, Gerry Adams, about his love of shrubs and trees – a subject a far cry from the battle for a united Ireland!

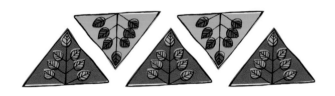

We all have certain shared experiences – families, children, homes, places we've travelled to, pets or hobbies. Choosing any one of these subjects to talk or ask questions about can create bridges, even in the most trying of circumstances. The spirit of *ubuntu* is at work here, when we reach out and find our common bonds to heal divisions or build new connections.

LEARN FROM OUR CHILDREN

Children and young people are the perfect candidates for teaching and inspiring us to see the basic good in people. With their natural energy, innocence and enthusiasm, they are often more accepting of people and situations than adults can be.

Not long ago, I heard a story on the news about a seven-year-old girl called Anu, from Birmingham in the West Midlands. She'd just been given a new pink sports blade, having lost a leg shortly after she was born. Growing up, she'd worn a prosthetic and now, for the first time, was going back to school with a state-of-the-art blade.

As the young girl rejoined her classmates in the playground, a TV crew filmed her. Her friends looked briefly at her new leg and shouted 'wow' in amazement. Then, all the children happily chased each other around, easily accepting Anu and her new leg.

'When we see the face of a child, we think of the future. We think of their dreams, about what they might become, and what they might accomplish.'

Archbishop Desmond Tutu

Young people have a natural positivity and energy to drive our world on to better things. They are our future, and with good education it's possible to change the way we live for the better. It's just one reason why the Tutu Foundation mainly works with younger people.

The Foundation itself has chosen to work in areas where young people are known to be struggling. We have sought out parts of the UK experiencing high levels of poverty and youth apathy, from London to Newcastle. We want to find those young people to whom nobody really makes the effort to talk. We want to see if we can give them a voice and hear what they have to say when, often, nobody else is listening.

To date, the programme has reached hundreds of kids across the country and has been rolled out across ten different London boroughs. The previously mentioned Ubuntu Round Table was developed with the Tutu Foundation by one such teenager, Blair, and his friend Mark.

The origins of the project stem from when Blair and his friends were regularly stopped and searched by police in London as teenagers. They were subjected to profiling by police that many classed as institutional racism. Often they were targeted simply because of how they looked. Rather than get weighed down by feelings of resentment and despair, Blair and his friends arranged to sit down with a group of police officers to explore their differences and find common ground.

The Tutu Foundation helped to develop this idea with him into the Ubuntu Round Table, where large groups of police officers and young people were brought together for an opportunity to talk, see past stereotypes and connect with each other.

We asked the police not to wear their uniforms to the event and to be as open and honest as possible, because we wanted the young people present to view them as individuals, not officers or figures of authority. The aim was to engineer a situation where both parties could find the 'good' in each other. Both sides needed to see the human being beyond the uniform or the hoodie; the essence of *ubuntu*.

PUTTING FAITH INTO *UBUNTU*

To begin with, all our young people were doubtful about speaking to the authorities they had grown up feeling wary of. So we enlisted the help of youth leaders who could help to build bridges and, through the process, many of the young people were surprised to discover the things they had in common with the officers. Several officers had grown up on rough estates just like these youngsters had, or experienced gang or drug crime. They also explained how they appreciated being able to find a safe space for young people's voices to be heard.

The aim had been to create a forum where young people could see the good in police and the police could see the good in the young people, and that both groups cared about the other's opinion – a message both sides rarely heard in society. The Round Table achieved just that. The results of the police and young people sitting and talking together were incredible. The teenagers were able to share stories of when police had been heavy handed with them and their friends, and how they didn't feel the police were on the side of young people. In turn, the officers shared their own personal stories.

One gave a harrowing account of when he was sent alone to a house to respond to a 999 call one evening. There, he found an appalling scene – a flat covered in blood. He described how it was the worst thing he'd ever experienced and was left shaken and unable to sleep.

Blair could see clearly how much the officer had been traumatized by the situation and was uncomfortable talking about it. As a result, while underlying issues remained, Blair was able to grasp his humanity. 'Police are just normal humans with feelings. I could then appreciate how difficult it is to be a police officer,' he told me.

The officer in question also shared how his eyes had been opened by Blair's perspective. 'I understand why some people may not want to talk to me given their previous experiences,' he said. 'I now understand how scary it is growing up in this day and age.'

Overall, the police officers came to a new understanding of why young people might not want to stop and speak to them on the streets.

Is it really possible to find good in *everyone*, though? At times it can be very challenging to choose to see the positives.

LOOK FOR THE GOOD AND YOU WILL FIND IT

Nelson Mandela's extraordinary reaction towards his prison guard on Robben Island lies at the heart of *ubuntu*. Christo Brand was just eighteen years old and pro-apartheid when he began work on the island, helping to keep Mandela under lock and key.

At first, Brand treated Mandela, then aged sixty, like any other prisoner, but he soon realized that wasn't sustainable. Years later, Brand told the *Observer*: 'He was down-to-earth and courteous. He treated me with respect and my respect for him grew. After a while, even though he was a prisoner, a friendship grew.'

This burgeoning friendship, nurtured across bars, went on to change Brand's life. Mandela saw him as a human being still, a man who needed a job even if it was one that dehumanized him. He talked to Brand with respect and asked him about his life, and found their common ground, until gradually a very unlikely connection developed. By the time Mandela was released, the pair were firm friends and Brand had completely changed his views on race and apartheid. Quietly and consistently, Mandela had chosen to see the good in his guard.

It takes strength and determination to see the good in someone we don't know, or someone we suspect might not have our best interests at heart. Forcing ourselves to look for the good in someone takes real character.

CONFRONT YOUR BIAS

Human beings are cursed with negativity bias, where our brains tend naturally to focus on the negatives. To overcome this bias we can decide to question it.

A famous Yoruba proverb says, 'If you damage the character of another, you damage your own.' That's to say, if we criticize and stand in judgement of others, we also hurt ourselves.

My grandfather was horrified by some of the graphic crimes he heard about during his time as chairman of the TRC, but it didn't stop him from believing in the good of the people who had perpetrated them. He took on board the fact that both black and white people were suffering, that nobody was spared, and he chose to acknowledge that people were giving testimony for the wider good of the nation, no matter how difficult it was to hear.

He believed you are not the worst thing you do in life and that nobody is born to hate anyone else. Everyone is capable of evil, we all have good and bad in us – the light and the dark – but *ubuntu* is when we choose to act on the good.

In everyday life, when we choose to see the good or bad in someone, whatever we decide is often reflected back to us. If you attack, you're likely to be attacked. If you approach someone with loving kindness, assuming the same will be returned to you, you're far more likely to experience that.

Psychologists call it our Reticular Activating System (RAS), a small part of our brain close to the top of the spinal column, which, among other things, helps us to direct our attention. If we focus on one particular thing – something negative, for example – then we will find more of it. If we focus on something positive, then we will also find more of it. If we believe young people wearing hoodies are trouble, for instance, our RAS will look for evidence of this.

Imagine you subscribe to this belief – that most young hoodie-wearers are up to no good. Now imagine seeing a cyclist wearing a hoodie and riding on the pavement near you. A whole wave of bad thoughts might begin to pass through your mind. If, on the other hand, we decide to look for the good, we might find ourselves thinking differently. We might consider that the young person is trying to cycle more safely because the traffic is fast-moving on that particularly busy stretch of road. We might also spot how they slowed down to allow us to pass. We might even consider that they are out running an errand for an elderly relative. We might also go so far as to make eye contact and notice them thanking us for stepping aside. We can instil kinder beliefs if we choose to look for them. The more we do so, the more we retrain our RAS to find the good in people.

Ubuntu reminds us to try to do this in all aspects of our daily lives. At work, it can help us to make progress with colleagues. Focusing on co-workers' strengths and talents will foster a positive work culture in which all can thrive. If your boss believes in you, you're far more likely to excel in your role than if he or she is actively looking for your mistakes and trying to catch you out. At home, if you believe in your children and reward them for good behaviour, they're more likely to behave well.

Ubuntu teaches us not to feel threatened by the good of others. Instead, we should seek it out and encourage those people to shine. That way we all bring out the best in one another.

See the good in yourself first of all. It stands to reason that if we berate ourselves constantly, we're more likely to act the same towards other people. If we find ourselves criticizing someone for doing a particular thing, we're unconsciously judging ourselves, because it's probably something we do too. We might look at someone and silently criticize their choice of outfit, for example, because we don't feel comfortable in what we put on that morning. We might judge someone for the way they made a speech, because deep down we know we'd be very afraid to stand up in front of a crowd of people and talk. Take the opportunity to catch yourself in the moment and ask if what you're really doing is mirroring something you don't like about yourself.

Think of someone you know but dislike. It could be a neighbour who plays loud music or an ex-partner who didn't treat you well. Perhaps it's someone who failed to repay some money you lent them. Then ask yourself, 'Were they always like this?' and 'What made them behave this way?' Perhaps the neighbour is going through a difficult time and isn't able to consider other people's feelings at the moment. Or did your ex behave badly because they were having a hard time at work or dealing with an ageing parent?

If we slow down and ask significant questions, we can begin to feel differently about someone. Approaching our relationships with compassion feels better for us and is more likely to create bonds with others. Acting from a place of anger gives off an energy which puts people on the defensive. No good can come of that.

Smile. A smile looks for the good in people. Such a small act is very powerful and often makes us feel good too. Think of Mandela, my grandfather, Obama and other great leaders, who all have many strengths in common, but one particular thing is their big smile. Smiling sends a message to other people that we are approachable, friendly and want to make a connection. Very often, a smile is infectious and is reflected back at us, putting everyone at ease.

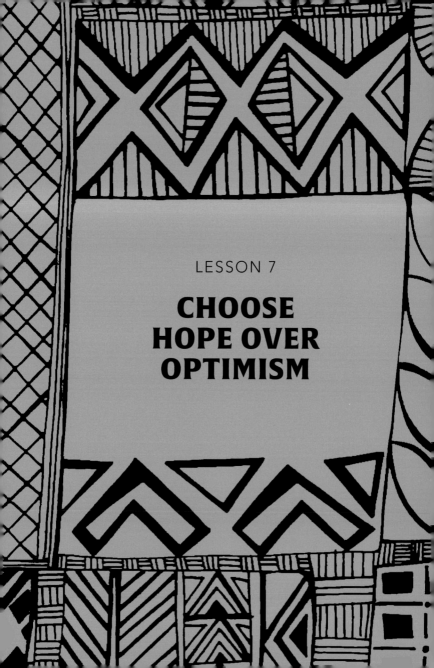

LESSON 7

CHOOSE
HOPE OVER
OPTIMISM

'We must accept finite disappointment but not lose infinite hope.'

Martin Luther King, Jr.

When we speak with *ubuntu* in mind, the words we choose to utter are important. My grandfather once said the word 'hope' is far more powerful than 'optimism'. Let's look at the definitions of the two.

'Hope' means 'the feeling of expectation and desire for a particular thing to happen and a feeling of trust' whereas the meaning of 'optimism' is 'hopefulness and confidence about the future or success of something'.

'Hope is being able to see that there is light despite all of the darkness.'

Archbishop Desmond Tutu

'Hope' requires trust and having faith. In this context, faith doesn't necessarily have to be of the religious kind. We can have faith in other people or our own abilities; in loved ones, ourselves, our doctors or our colleagues. Hope means that we haven't given up. It's a sensibility, an energy within that informs our lives. We live in hope and hold on to it. Often, when people lose hope it means they have given up completely.

Optimism, on the other hand, is a feeling, and feelings come and go. Optimism can change into pessimism when the going gets tough because it is based on circumstances. We don't say 'where there is life, there is optimism', we say 'where there is life, there is hope.'

My grandfather had hope during the worst of the struggle against apartheid. Optimism is more likely to leave a person when they're in the darkest of places, whereas hope is a light that burns bright and keeps us going in the face of adversity.

We say 'don't give up hope' even in the most desperate of situations because we've all heard stories of defying the odds. We've all seen it happen. It could have been a loved one overcoming a terminal diagnosis or a previously infertile friend conceiving a baby. We've all watched documentaries of incredible feats of human endurance where survivors refused to give up, or people battled for justice.

Ubuntu recognizes that life isn't always easy. More realistically, it tells us that even when we're suffering in the darkness, and times are really tough, we are still human and still deserving of light. Whoever we are. And if we seek inspiration elsewhere and open our hearts to others, we're much more likely to find it.

THE STRENGTH IN HOPE

During many political processes, especially those involved in trying to broker peace deals, hope is something everyone needs to agree to believe in. Often at the beginning of the process, when warring parties appear to have nothing in common, that is all there is. A hope that this too shall pass.

Lord Peter Hain told me that during the Northern Ireland peace process, the then prime minister, Tony Blair, held an 'absolutely unshakeable belief' it could be and had to be resolved. Blair made finding peace in Northern Ireland a priority right from his very first day in office in May 1997. Without a doubt, this hope played a big part in the eventual success of the Good Friday Agreement.

On a smaller scale, ordinary people vocalizing their hope can inspire others to persist in trying to create a future worth having. In 1992, during the Balkan conflict, Scottish brothers Magnus and Fergus MacFarlane-Barrow had the idea to organize an appeal for blankets and food to help the people of Bosnia-Herzegovina. Magnus and various volunteers drove the supplies to Medjugorje, the region in need. When he returned home to Argyll, donations kept flooding in. Unexpectedly, Magnus never went back to his job as a fish farmer. Instead, his work providing aid to different parts of the world grew.

In 2002, Magnus met a family in Malawi whose own hopes and dreams set in motion an opportunity to change thousands of lives. In a hut, sitting on the ground, Magnus met Emma, a mother who was dying of AIDS as her six children sat round her. Magnus asked her eldest son, Edward, what his hopes were in life. Edward replied, 'To have enough to eat and to go to school one day.'

These 'hopes' stayed in Magnus's mind. He didn't give up his own hope to make a better life for the people he had met, because they hadn't given up on themselves. Two hundred children in Malawi began to receive a nutritious daily school lunch later that year, thanks to Magnus and his work. Now, seventeen years later, Mary's Meals is a global charity, providing daily school meals for more than 1.4 million children in eighteen different countries.

During the worst of times, hope is often the only thing left and can be the difference between life and death. Nelson Mandela spent twenty-seven years in jail as a political prisoner on the notorious Robben Island in abysmal conditions. While he was incarcerated, his mother died and his son was killed in a car crash. He wasn't permitted to attend either funeral. He lived day to day in a cramped, eight-by-seven-foot cell and was only allowed outside to carry out hard labour quarrying limestone. He was bullied by guards and suffered damage to his eyesight from the glare of the sun against the rocks. And yet he never gave up hope.

Mandela is remembered for many things but hope is one of his defining characteristics. In letters to his wife, Winnie, Mandela talked about his feelings on the matter: 'Remember that hope is a powerful weapon even when all else is lost.' After Mandela's death in 2013, Barack Obama said that he had given him 'a sense of what human beings can do when they are guided by their hopes and not their fears.'

Whoever we are and whatever we want to achieve from life, we're going to have a better experience if we follow our hopes (and dreams) rather than be hindered by fear.

NURTURE HOPE IN YOUR LIFE

Hope will follow once we invite *ubuntu* into our lives. We will err towards a hopeful stance because others will inspire us to seek out the positive. It is a fundamental and natural part of human nature. Everywhere we look there are everyday examples of hope in action. We get married because we believe in love and have the hope it will work out. We have children in the hope they will survive and reach adulthood and live happily. If we choose to do charitable work, we do so hoping to make a difference in the world.

Making an effort to nurture our human inclination to hope is a powerful way to help achieve our ambitions in life. As with every goal we aim for, there will be a challenge. Nobody's path runs smoothly. It's during these times our resolve is tested, but if we believe in hope we gain a sense of resilience.

Dr Valerie Maholmes, from the Yale Child Study Center, revealed poor children who managed to succeed in life all had one factor in common: hope. Success in the study included academic achievement or overcoming economic, social and health barriers, such as finding gainful employment, staying out of gangs or managing health problems. She discovered if children used strategies such as learning to cope with difficult emotions and used talking therapies, they were more likely to thrive and succeed in adulthood. We are more likely to seek and find a solution if we have hope. It drives us forward even when we might feel like giving up, and as we hope for something better, that propels us to achieve.

As Mandela recognized from his own experience, hope works in the face of extreme conditions too. It might be the loss of a loved one or a job, the illness of a child, or even the loss of our way of life and our liberty.

In 1985, Anthony Ray Hinton was arrested for multiple murders and robberies in Birmingham, Alabama. He'd been set up by police. At his trial, evidence was withheld and he was imprisoned and placed in solitary confinement on death row for thirty years, despite being an innocent man.

Hinton described the Alabama prison that became his home as a hell on earth. Men shared cells with rats and cockroaches, were given very little to eat, and were only allowed out of their cells for fifteen minutes each day. From down the corridor, they heard the sounds of death, and smelled it too as their neighbours or cellmates, one by one, were burned alive on the electric chair.

It was a place where many men quickly lost all hope. Suicides were common or men gave up and succumbed to mental health problems. Hinton clung on. Helped by a friend who never failed to visit him once a week, and a belief that one day the truth would prevail, he never lost hope.

Thirty years after he was wrongly imprisoned and placed on death row, Hinton was exonerated. He was released on 3 April 2015. Hope and justice did prevail. In his memoir published soon after his release, he wrote, 'Despair was a choice. Hatred was a choice. Anger was a choice. I still had choices and that knowledge rocked me . . . I could choose to give up or to hang on. Hope was a choice. Faith was a choice. And more than anything love was a choice.'

POSSIBILITIES IN PROJECTION

Whatever our circumstances we can always choose hope. Hope for a better future can help our present difficulties to appear temporary.

This ability to project into the future is a key component of the power of hope. If there is nothing else you can do to improve your situation, you can at least allow yourself to *imagine* things working out for you. This positive energy can then begin to alleviate the turmoil. Allowing yourself to imagine the best-case scenario, rather than the worst, provides relief. Hope grows if you pay attention to it but it can die if you suppress it with negative thoughts or cynicism.

Bryan Stevenson is a US lawyer who works tirelessly for prisoners via his not-for-profit charity, Equal Justice Initiative. In his book *Just Mercy* he talks about the importance of hope against great odds. He says he often mentions Václav Havel, the Czech leader who said 'hope' was what people who struggled in Eastern Europe during the Soviet era needed. Havel mentioned that people wanted things such as independence, money and support from the outside world, but hope was what they had and that's what made all the difference.

'Not that pie in the sky stuff,' Stevenson writes. 'Not a preference for optimism over pessimism, but rather an "orientation of the spirit". The kind of hope that creates a willingness to position oneself in a hopeless place and be a witness, that allows one to believe in a better future, even in the face of abusive power. The kind of hope that makes one strong.'

Ubuntu teaches us that the power of hope is contagious too. If our families or friends are suffering, we can talk positively from a place of hope to help them. It's more than simply looking on the bright side; it's assuring them that we have faith that things will improve.

Hope is there for us all to find, if we look for it.

What to do if all hope feels lost. Life tests us, sometimes beyond our resolve. Especially if we are tired, hungry, unwell or feeling alone, problems can feel overwhelming. Surviving these lows is about finding hope again and reaching out to embrace concepts of ubuntu. Here are some ideas for when a sense of hopelessness has taken over.

1. **Accept the situation.** This is the way you're feeling, so honour it – cry and release your emotions. *Ubuntu* tells us that we need to take care of ourselves and be honest about our feelings. This helps to identify why you're feeling hopeless. Is it because of a recent upset? Or is it a long-term struggle? Whatever it is, naming the reasons for your feelings will help you to release them.

2. **Take action.** Some call it 'wallowing' but hopelessness can easily feel like a spiral into which you're sucked and out of which it is impossible to pull yourself. You feel lethargic, unmotivated and in despair. Listen to your internal dialogue. It might contain phrases such as, 'but I can't', 'there's no point' or 'I've already tried'. The first step is turning those words around and changing every negative into a positive. Say these new phrases out loud – 'I can', 'I won't give up' and 'I'll try again' all send a powerful message to our subconscious.

3. **Live in the present moment.** Do something to make yourself feel better physically, even if you're struggling mentally – the two are linked. A long brisk walk, calling a positive friend, eating wholesome food. These are all small things we can do to help change our immediate concerns. Worrying is wishing for what you don't want to happen, so don't agonize over the future. Focus on the present. Do anything that takes you out of yourself, even if it's just for a few moments.

4. **Write a gratitude list.** *Ubuntu* shows us that we all have something for which to be grateful, so now is the time to examine the good stuff in detail. You might be thankful for your physical health, your family, caring friends, the delicious cup of coffee you're drinking. Name the things you feel good about right now. It's an exercise that will shift your mood, energetically and quickly.

5. **Set goals.** If you've reached a place of desperate hopelessness, you need to put in work each day to overcome the feeling. Get going by setting yourself new goals, and begin with very small ones – incremental and easy-to-achieve steps.

If you've lost your job, start by reaching out to trusted contacts for advice, then build up to looking at job adverts before applying for positions. If you've been ditched by a partner, give yourself time to grieve and talk things through with a counsellor or friend. Allow yourself space to heal before even thinking about dating again. If you're in despair because you've gained weight, find a simple exercise app to inspire you, build up the amount of exercise you do every day, find a workout buddy, then look at food plans to help you make a bigger transformation. Small steps help hope to gather momentum.

6. **Find your faith.** This could be a long-term goal that evolves over time. It doesn't have to be a religious faith, but having faith in something you can trust is something *everyone* needs. It could be faith in your abilities or your choices. You could put your faith in going for a daily run to improve your mental health or in eating nutritious food so that you have energy for the day.

Build some of these hopeful ideas into a new daily routine. They'll bolster you and give you an inner strength and hope on which to rely when things become difficult.

LESSON 8

SEEK OUT
WAYS TO
CONNECT

'Birds sing not because they have the answers but because they have songs.'

African proverb

It is human nature to feel disconnected from life at times. Feelings of isolation, apathy or loneliness can sometimes overwhelm us. Especially when we're stressed, tired or anxious. Instead of hiding away, *ubuntu* tells us we should reach out to humanity during these testing periods and allow ourselves to be comforted by it. And there are many ways of doing this.

Art is one way we can place ourselves in a different frame of mind. A human being's desire to be heard and to communicate through different art forms dates back to the Stone Age. Some of the earliest prints are from 40,000 BC, when shapes and pictures of animals were drawn. One especially resonant picture of lots of handprints was found on a cave wall near Perito Moreno, Argentina, and looks as though hands from the past are waving to say hello. It's a nice idea.

Art, music and literature made by other humans, as well as the beauty of nature, can lift our spirits, make us feel heard, understood or refreshed. Many art forms can even articulate feelings we find hard to verbalize. Have you ever stood in front of a particular painting and been struck by the way it makes you feel? Or read an inspirational quote and been inspired by the words? Or listened to music and felt your spirits rise? Sometimes we have to look beyond our comfort zone in order to reconnect with the things that matter.

In 1999, Dumi Senda came from Zimbabwe to work in the UK as a youth leader but also loved to write poetry, especially around the subject of *ubuntu*. Afraid of being laughed at, he never showed his writing to anyone and kept it hidden under his bed.

Five years after arriving in the UK, Dumi faced the stress of not knowing whether his visa was going to be renewed. Depressed and isolated, he stayed at home waiting for news, immersing himself in his writing. During this difficult period, he heard about a Zimbabwean business meeting being held near his home in London and, on a whim, Dumi asked to attend. When asked what his business was, he admitted he didn't have one, but confessed that he did write poetry. To his surprise, the organizer invited him along to represent the creative industries.

'Art is man's constant effort to create for himself a different order of reality from that which is given to him.'

Chinua Achebe

Dumi agreed but then immediately regretted it. He'd never shown anyone his poetry before, much less read it aloud in public. What if people laughed? What if he was humiliated? Despite his misgivings he went along, shaking with nerves as he stood in front of the crowd and read out his words.

The audience's response went way beyond his wildest dreams. Not only did people applaud, they approached him afterwards to congratulate him and encourage him to continue. The confidence boost from sharing his poetry led to him feeling connected in a way he'd never experienced before. Connections come from vulnerability, and Dumi embraced vulnerability when he chose to share the art that was close to his heart.

Dumi continued writing and, just a few years later, his work was published. Now an internationally acclaimed poet, he has even performed in honour of Mandela by invitation of the BBC and been a guest speaker at the United Nations. From that single opportunity that he bravely pursued, he discovered his art was good enough to share. The rewards were life-changing.

THE JOY OF JOINING IN

Music and song have been proven to help us feel united and are also good for our health. Nowhere is this more evident than when it comes to singing in a choir. Scientific research has shown that choral singing is beneficial both psychologically and physically.

Several studies have revealed the act increases oxygen levels in our bodies, boosts immunity, lowers blood pressure, regulates hormones and can even help stroke victims' damaged brains to heal. One study from Oxford University found taking part in the active performance of music also generates endorphins, which elevate our pain threshold.

It's one reason why joining a choir is promoted as a remedy for people suffering from mental health issues. Music is a way of communicating emotions and singing in unison helps us bond on a primal level, boosting feelings of inspiration and happiness. Even when watching a live show, the audience members feel as one, because we all appreciate the moment together. It's *ubuntu* – a sense of community – in the form of entertainment and joy.

Sport is another unifying force across the world, with football being the most popular. Globally it's estimated that 4 billion people support or watch the game, whose roots have been traced back as far as second-century China.

As with music, the feel-good factor is the reason behind sport's popularity. Being a fan of a team makes you a member of a community and instantly provides a sense of belonging. A study by researchers at Nottingham Trent University asked 4,000 people how connected they felt to their local community and family. There was a clear link between happiness levels and those who had an association with other groups, such as a sports team or a choir.

Sport can also transcend generations, as the love of a game is often shared within families – passed down from grandparents to grandchildren – and provides a constant in people's lives. If you support a team, you can do so from childhood to adulthood. There are few other things in life that last as long. Or you could be like my family, and enjoy a little bit of healthy competition where we all support different teams in the Premier League! But for us it's still a connection.

For male sports fans in particular, a game can provide an important outlet for the expression of emotions. Dr Alan Pringle from Nottingham University conducted a study of fans from one English club and confirmed this to be the case. In an article which appeared in the *Huffington Post*, he wrote: 'Football offers a safe space where expressed emotion is acceptable (even crying or hugging other men!).' The downside is disappointment if you lose, but if you win you share a victory. Cheering at the top of your lungs is a release like no other.

Supporting a team also gives individuals the sense of having others on your side, and this is why a decision made by Nelson Mandela to support the Springboks made history. Shortly after becoming president, Mandela used the final of the 1995 Rugby World Cup – the first major sporting event to take place in South Africa following the end of apartheid – to make a breakthrough with hardline white South Africans.

The match took place between the South African Springboks, widely viewed as a white elitist side, and New Zealand's All Blacks at Ellis Park in Johannesburg. At the time, the green-and-yellow Springbok jersey was seen as a symbol of privilege and the oppression of black people, and it was widely hated. As rugby was considered to be an Afrikaner sport, some black South Africans even made a point of cheering for the opposing team. So what Mandela did next was inspired.

When South Africa won the match, Mandela wore the Springbok shirt and cap as he walked on to the field to present the cup to the Springbok captain, Francois Pienaar – a white, blond-haired Afrikaner. The look on Pienaar's face was one of amazement and tears pricked his eyes. The white Afrikaner crowd went wild, cheering to see their former enemy dressed in their clothing. Mandela's message was loud and clear; he was at one with everyone, including his past oppressors. His choice to wear that jersey displayed *ubuntu*.

The image of him wearing the team's shirt was beamed around the world. It was a match that brought both sides of the country together and went a long way to helping to heal the Rainbow Nation's deep wounds.

THE KEY TO CONNECTION IS EDUCATION

Reading books connects us to bigger ideas and concepts, and teaches us about the wider world. From works of literature, we can realize that the same human characteristics, and the same trials and tribulations we face today, were experienced centuries ago. There's something profoundly comforting about this. Whether you're learning about love from Jane Austen writing in the 1800s or gaining an insight into betrayal from Shakespeare's *Hamlet*, written in around 1600, literature teaches us about the human condition. Spoiler alert: it hasn't changed much.

The most popular books are well loved because they cross the space and time divide and 'speak' to us, whoever we are. Once we pick up a good book we find it hard to put down, as the feeling of being understood and connected to a powerful story is addictive – we want to consume more.

Books help us to understand others and make sense of our own lives.

'Education is the most powerful weapon you can use to change the world,' said Mandela.

The Lapdesk Company was founded by Shane Immelman, and is part of a project to encourage learning across Africa. Over 95 million children in schools across the continent have no access to a classroom desk, and these portable lapdesks made by the company are manufactured from durable, recyclable materials designed to last for a child's whole school career.

'It's the storyteller who makes us who we are, who creates history.'

Chinua Achebe

In 2008 it was renamed Tutudesk when my grandfather became the company's patron and pledged to provide 20 million desks across the continent by 2025. Tutudesks help unite and connect classes of students, wherever they may be, by allowing kids to sit anywhere and hold a functioning class. They make learning easier and exam results show that literacy skills have already improved significantly. It's just a simple thing, but it makes a big difference and brings a sense of *ubuntu* into the lives of children who might not otherwise have easy access to the joy of learning.

LOOK OUTSIDE TO SEE
THE CONNECTION

Nature is another powerful force with the ability to unite us. And it's free. Gazing up at the stars and moon on a pitch-dark night, admiring a sunset over an ocean, the smell of woodland after the rain . . . These are all things which universally engage our senses.

Study after study has shown that being outside in the natural world makes us feel energized and more positive. One such report from Sweden in 1993 revealed that when heart surgery patients in recovery were shown pictures of the natural world in a window view, an abstract art work and a blank wall, those who were shown the water and tree scenes were less anxious and needed less pain relief.

For me, the beach is my chosen place of escape. The sea is a perfect illustration of how life often feels: overwhelming and unknown, yet really exciting. To be thrown around by the waves makes you feel like a child again, with no responsibilities except enjoying the ocean in that moment. For the time you're in the water, you're at one with nature. Nature has the upper hand, of course. The size and ferocity of the sea can make you realize how small we are and that we are no more than part of a much bigger system. When you sit and stare at the ocean it's amazing to think about being able to swim in such a vast body of water. In this moment of serenity I also think of those who might be thinking the exact same thing when they too experience the ocean.

Less physical but challenging in other ways, gardening appeals to many people as a way to stay in close touch with the natural world. It provides physical exercise and it's creative. Sunshine and natural daylight are known to help improve our mental health. There's even evidence from the Food Growing in Schools Taskforce Report, led by charity Garden Organic, that children who take part in growing programmes in schools exhibit improved behaviour, raised self-esteem and go on to develop a more positive attitude to eating healthily.

'No man fears what he has seen grown.'

African proverb

Ubuntu tells us that in order to feel human we need to feel connected. A sense of togetherness is necessary to find contentment and satisfaction in everyday life. We can reach out to our fellow men and women to feel part of something more than ourselves, but there are also other, quieter ways to connect – such as sitting in a tree-lined park or swimming in the outdoors – that are just as beneficial. If you find yourself alone, for whatever reason, positive or negative, try experimenting with something new today that will allow you to reconnect in a way all humans can appreciate.

Discover yourself through a journal. Julia Cameron, author of *The Artist's Way*, advises we take some time first thing in the morning to write our stream of consciousness in 'morning pages'. The words don't have to make perfect sense but they can help us reconnect to what we're feeling inside. The aim is not to write a novel or poetry but to purge whatever thoughts we have for release in a cathartic stream of consciousness. Don't overthink it. Write down what is on your mind and let it all go. Julia also advises we do this before looking at any screens!

Communicate clearly to have your basic needs met. If you don't feel appreciated, wanted or listened to, then it's time to speak out. It isn't always easy but it can help to make change happen. Think about what it is that's upset you, then decide you're the master of this feeling so it's up to you to do something about it. Next, try to communicate clearly how you're feeling and what it is you're not receiving. Perhaps your partner isn't treating you well, or your work colleague isn't pulling their weight. Be very specific about what other people can do to help you.

Let yourself be vulnerable. If we open ourselves up to experiencing connections, we can feel emotional. This is good. If you're supporting your favourite team, cheer and shout and enjoy the moment. If you're listening to music, allow yourself to connect with the lyrics or feel uplifted by

the crescendo, which can be a powerful experience when we're feeling sad. Equally, if you're reaching out to a friend or loved one to have your needs met, allow yourself to show how you're feeling. From vulnerability comes a sense of authenticity that others often respond to positively. If you open up, others are more likely to want to be around you. With vulnerability comes an opportunity to connect deeply.

Connecting to creativity. Human beings love to create. In our most inspired moments, we can enter a state of 'flow', which is when we're lost in what we're doing. We're truly connected. Try five things to find your flow again.

1. Get away from the computer, including social media.

2. Visit somewhere near by you've never been before, or look up a local exhibition or a place of interest.

3. Buy a cheap pad of blank paper and allow yourself to doodle, collect your favourite quotes or jot down ideas.

4. Do something with your hands. It could be making a cake, planting seeds in the garden, or playing with Play-Doh with (or even without!) the kids. Allow yourself to become absorbed in the moment and take delight in it.

5. Find inspiration from outside yourself. Look up artists you love, borrow a book by your favourite author from the library, watch the TEDx series of talks on creativity.

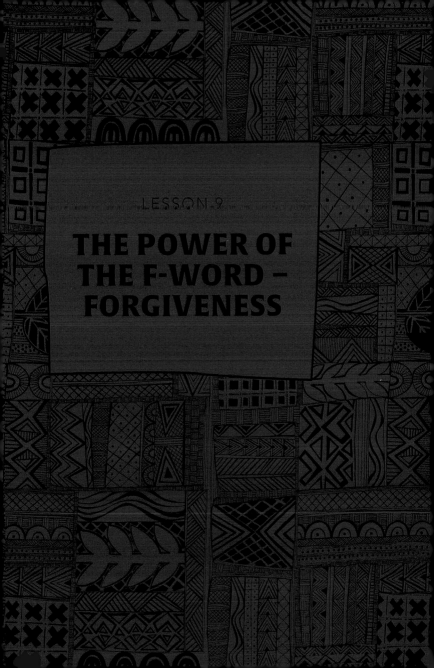

THE POWER OF THE F-WORD – FORGIVENESS

'The weak can never forgive.
Forgiveness is the attribute
of the strong.'

Mahatma Gandhi

Forgiveness can mean different things to different people. For some, it is a one-off decision, something we make a choice to do in the spur of the moment and then move on from. It might be in response to a minor incident, such as a work colleague forgetting to prepare something vital for a meeting, or a teacher who accidentally marks an exam paper incorrectly. It's a decision that's easy to make.

However, for bigger wrongs against us, forgiveness can be a painful journey where the decision to forgive needs to be made several times along the way. It can take resilience and courage to do.

Ubuntu tells us forgiveness can give us back our self-respect and dignity. The spirit of *ubuntu* counsels reaching outwards and teaches us that it's not good to sit alone with the pain of bitterness. It demonstrates that forgiveness serves us well – not only as individuals but in our communities too. It returns peace of mind to the person who is angered and brings peace to all our lives.

Forgiveness is a central tenet of the Christian faith, but whether you have religious beliefs or not, it doesn't matter. On a psychological level, making the choice to absolve someone is a cathartic process and can benefit anyone. We can be inspired by other people in the wider world who have forgiven acts against them, offences often far more serious than the slights we ourselves have suffered.

However, while forgiveness is an easy thing to talk about, it's one of the hardest things to actually do.

THE CHALLENGES OF FORGIVING

Pride and self-righteousness can often hold us back. When someone has wronged us, we feel justified in our anger, hurt and unease. This is especially so if the person who has wounded us shows no understanding or remorse for their actions. 'If this individual has injured me, why *shouldn't* I hold it against them?' It's a natural human reaction.

Perhaps being angry for a day, a week or a month is justified. But what about big hurts from the past that we've all experienced and are unable to let go of? When a loved one betrayed us. When a parent let us down. When someone committed a criminal act against us. When an organization failed us in a way that changed our life for the worse. What happens if we choose *not* to forgive?

**'Bitterness is like a cancer,
it eats upon the host.'**

Maya Angelou

When we don't forgive, we ourselves suffer. If we replay in our minds the feeling or incident that hurt us in the first place and tap into bitterness, it feels tortuous, because

THE POWER OF THE F-WORD – FORGIVENESS

bitterness keeps pain alive. Often it is something we hold on to in private while we harbour the deep-rooted hurt. We feel justified for doing so, but if we choose to do this we end up trapped in our painful past. An unforgiving nature doesn't give our anger anywhere to go.

Choosing not to forgive can cloud our judgement of other people too. If one partner has betrayed you, you might become suspicious of all future lovers. If a work colleague has spread malicious gossip about you, you might believe you'll never work in a harmonious environment again.

We can't change the events of our past, and very often we can't take revenge against the person who has harmed us (*ubuntu* tells us that this would be even more damaging, in any case). As a result, we suffer by reliving the hurt again and again. So how do we forgive when we still feel the after-effects of the offending actions? It can seem as if a super-human effort is required. It can seem impossible.

FORGIVING THE UNFORGIVABLE

Ingrid von Stein, former communications director for the Desmond Tutu Peace Centre, made an amazing decision to forgive what appeared to be an unforgivable act. In the mid 1980s – about a decade before she began working with my grandfather – she was brutally attacked by four youths in an assault that almost destroyed her. The men were arrested and sent to jail, but for many years Ingrid found herself completely preoccupied by negative feelings towards them.

She was filled with rage about what had happened, but suffered in silence. She felt she couldn't tell anyone because she didn't want to be known as the woman who had been attacked. She didn't want everyone to look at her differently.

So Ingrid harboured her bitterness in secret and even felt ashamed about it.

Then, one day, Ingrid was chatting with my grandfather, just as two friends. My grandfather had been having a difficult time and had decided to confide in her when, all of a sudden, he said, 'Ingrid, we are like identical twins!'

She laughed and asked him why. Physically, they couldn't be less alike, and she pointed out their very different appearances.

'Exactly!' he cried. 'We are identical!'

What he meant by this was, despite their physical differences, they were both human beings who'd suffered pain.

In this moment of closeness with my grandfather, feeling able to unburden herself, Ingrid poured out her feelings towards her attackers. She felt trapped by her hurt and anger. She didn't know what to do or who to turn to. My grandfather agreed that she had every right to feel angry about the actions of the men, but he also implored her to try to move past the incident and forgive them.

To Ingrid this was anathema. How on earth could she forgive when she had been caused such physical and mental anguish? It was impossible. Over the next few months, the pair had many more conversations about it and then, one day, my grandfather asked her, 'Have you ever thought how the attackers might be feeling?'

Ingrid was furious, but my grandfather stayed calm. He explained that she had to let her anger out, but she also had to remember that her perpetrators were *just people too*.

Steadfast in her belief that she could never see the good in these people, Ingrid struggled to see how she could move on. It was then that my grandfather helped her get in touch with the institution that works in the prison system to facilitate reconciliations.

'Who forgives wins.'

African proverb

Feeling trapped by her own pain, Ingrid agreed to meet her attackers in a facilitated meeting. She had refused to see all four men at once, but two were not interested in meeting with her at all, so she focused, one at a time, on the remaining pair. Talking things through with my grandfather, Ingrid decided she didn't care whether they apologized or not. She simply wanted to try to see them as people.

Bravely, she met one of the men. Trembling, she sat down in front of him, uncertain about what would follow. However, as soon as she looked into his eyes, she saw a man – a human being – staring back at her.

They started to talk. Ingrid heard how this man had grown up in a drug-ridden, poverty-stricken block in Cape Town. His whole childhood had been marred by violence and abuse. It was a very different upbringing to her own, but she also identified similarities. Both their parents had abused alcohol and there were few boundaries. The man had been used as a punchbag as a child, just as Ingrid had been by her own father. For the first time, Ingrid saw her attacker as someone to whom she could relate.

Ingrid walked away from the conversation with her mind reeling. She'd reached out thinking she was unable to forgive, but she found herself feeling something she imagined impossible beforehand: compassion for her attacker.

After a similar conversation with the other member of the gang, Ingrid was flooded with a sense of relief, which she eventually recognized as forgiveness. She told me that leaving those bags at the door has made travelling through the rest of her life a much lighter experience, and a pleasure once again.

FACES OF FORGIVENESS

Our wider community can help us to forgive, but we should also respect ourselves enough to do so at our own pace. Nobody should feel forced to do it. It requires mental strength and has to be authentic – a respectful act that comes from within. Similarly, if we've slighted someone else and ask for their forgiveness, we mustn't assume we're entitled to it. We shouldn't expect forgiveness from other people so that we feel better.

When we forgive, we do so not for the sake of the person who has harmed us, but for our own sake.

The TRC was a profound example of how transparency was rolled out on a scale never seen before. It had its basis in this: the truth, all of it, is needed for forgiveness to really take hold. It was a dark time in South Africa's history and wasn't an easy process. At times, people felt unable to forgive someone directly, but this is where the TRC came into its own. It stood as a symbol of forgiveness, allowing a nation to move on, even if individuals continued to struggle to forgive. However, the Commission wasn't telling people simply to forget actions of the past and move on; it was encouraging people to listen to the whole story for the sake of the nation.

Matthew Goniwe was one of the so-called Cradock Four, named for the town from which the four men came, and whose story was one told in the film *Long Night's Journey into Day*.

In 1985, along with the anti-apartheid activists Fort Calata, Sparrow Mkhonto and Sicelo Mhlauli, Matthew was stopped at a roadblock by security police outside Port Elizabeth, killed and then burned. Goniwe was a popular teacher and community leader, and there was outcry at what had happened.

At the TRC, Afrikaner police officer Eric Taylor, who was responsible for the killings, told how he was one of five officers who ordered the men out of the car at the roadblock. They were then struck at the base of their skulls with an iron object and their bodies were set alight.

At the Commission, Taylor spoke about his part in the murders, and of his warped view that he had felt justified going after the men because they were 'godless' communists. He told how he had seen the error of his ways after watching the film *Mississippi Burning*.

This testimony gave scant comfort to Matthew's

devastated wife, Nyameka Goniwe. In *Long Night's Journey into Day*, directed by Frances Reid and Deborah Hoffmann, Nyameka says: 'I am not going to absolve him. If he wants to feel lighter, I am not the person to do that. He can use the Truth and Reconciliation Commission for that.' Her point was that while she cannot forgive Taylor directly, she had respect for the TRC and what it was trying to achieve.

It's important to note that forgiveness is not only emotionally uplifting but is also good for our health. Anger, resentment, rage and bitterness have a physical impact on the body. These negative emotions hamper our immune system, leaving us more vulnerable to illness, and also increase our chances of suffering from post-traumatic stress disorder, a condition that develops after a physical or emotional trauma and triggers our fight-or-flight response.

PTSD symptoms can include insomnia, angry outbursts, numbness and both psychological and physical tension. Studies have shown that learning to forgive, or agreeing to keep trying to forgive, can alleviate these symptoms. Simply put, forgiveness helps us to live happier, healthier lives.

FORGIVENESS = A FUTURE

If you're struggling with wanting to forgive, or feeling unable to do so, you can look to others for inspiration. *Ubuntu* is about seeing yourself in others, after all, so look to them for encouragement when you cannot do something alone.

Nelson Mandela is a clear example of a man able to forgive what appeared to be unforgivable acts against him. When he was asked to provide a list of people he wished to invite to his inauguration dinner as president of South Africa, he insisted his former jailer Christo Brand was invited, much to some people's surprise. By then, he and Christo had become good friends. This relationship was public knowledge and allowed other people in South Africa to reconsider whether they were able to forgive perpetrators of harm in their own lives.

'Without forgiveness there is no future.'

Archbishop Desmond Tutu

There is no 'one size fits all' when it comes to forgiveness. It can come in many forms – face-to-face or even symbolically.

Forgiveness was also necessary on a huge scale in Rwanda, following the genocide there. People were left with their hearts and minds feeling tortured by the unspeakable things that had happened. Many had lost loved ones in brutal acts of violence, often right in front of their eyes.

The very idea of forgiveness was unthinkable for many, but for some it became possible through a project called Cows for Peace. Founder Christophe Mbonyingabo explained to me how, in Rwanda, a cow is seen as a great gift from one person to another. The animals are symbols of wealth and prosperity, and in this instance the cow became a symbol of forgiveness too.

Cows need tending, often by whole families, so caring for one was a meaningful way of bringing people together again. Aided by the charity Tearfund, a survivor and offender worked together to look after the animal. Only then was the victim encouraged to 'gift' the cow to the perpetrator as an act of forgiveness.

The project was so successful that warring neighbours who had felt unable to speak to each other for decades found themselves talking again. These success stories helped to inspire the wider community too. The more people watched forgiveness in action, happening right before their eyes, the more likely they were to forgive too.

YOU ARE ONLY HUMAN, SO IT'S TIME TO FORGIVE *YOU*

Many people who test our boundaries, whether ex-partners, toxic parents, unsympathetic bosses or petty neighbours, don't suddenly become angels overnight. If you have someone in your life whose behaviours challenge you, but whom you need to live alongside, then forgiveness might be an ongoing act. Or you might feel the need to introduce boundaries to stop yourself from being hurt again. But what's even harder at times is forgiving ourselves, especially if we regret our past mistakes.

This might have been an unhappy life choice. You chose a job that didn't suit you, you wasted several years with a partner who eroded your self-esteem, you made a decision that led to a chain of events that hurt you. The list of things which can and do go wrong in our lives is endless.

But this is the point. We all make mistakes. It's human nature. We say to each other 'you're only human' when we mean you're liable to mess up, just like everyone else.

We should embrace our humanity and not deny it, and mistakes are part of being human. Few people knowingly choose the wrong path. We make decisions based on the best knowledge at the time. I chose to study at a college where I thought I'd be happy, but was proven wrong so had to start again. I didn't make that life choice on purpose, though.

We're often able to look at our friends and loved ones' life mistakes with an eye of forgiveness, so we should view our own missteps in the same way. If you're still feeling tortured and can't forgive yourself for the wrongs, then ask yourself this: did you make your bad choices *intentionally*? The answer is very likely to be no. If you did self-sabotage, then ask yourself this: why do you think you did this? Allow yourself time to reflect.

Forgiveness is complicated. We should even forgive ourselves for *wanting but struggling* to forgive. Remember that with *ubuntu* close to our hearts, anything is possible.

If you're holding a painful grudge and don't feel you can forgive, here are some ideas to help kickstart the process. It can initially feel as painful as the wound caused, but the effort is worth it in the long run.

1. **Forgive yourself first.** Are you angry with someone for hurting you? Do you burn with justification for feeling this way? Allow yourself to experience these emotions. Set aside half an hour to write down all the things about which you feel wronged. Make a note of what the other person did, how you felt afterwards, and the negative emotions you're holding on to. Read it aloud. Then tell yourself that you forgive yourself for feeling this way. And, if it helps, throw the piece of paper away. Do this whenever the anger you're feeling is disruptive.

2. **Think of all the advantages of forgiving.** Would you feel physically relieved? Would you stop ruminating on what the other person has done and free up some headspace? Would you be happier if you escaped your anger? Once you are sure the path of forgiveness is right for you, it's time to move on to the next stage.

3. **Working towards forgiving.** If you now feel that forgiveness might be a simpler process, try lighting a candle, thinking of the person who harmed you, and saying aloud, 'I love you, I forgive you and I am sorry for harbouring resentment.' If you know that forgiveness will be a harder process, delve more deeply into how you will forgive. Think of walking in the other person's shoes, the essence of *ubuntu*. Think of the person's life situation, why they have

made the choices they have. Making the effort to see things from their perspective often shifts angry energy into empathy.

4. **Accept it can take time.** If you choose to speak directly to the person in question, first let go of any expectation that they will react well to you offering your forgiveness. They might not apologize. They might not show respect for your decision. As you've reminded them of their poor behaviour, they might choose not to speak to you again. That's all OK. If you don't expect anything, you're less likely to feel hurt or disappointed by their actions or inactions. Make the act of forgiveness about *you*, and if the other side shows grace, then see it as a bonus.

5. **Keep going.** Forgiveness can be a two-way street or a one-way street – it doesn't matter which. If your old wounds surface again, go back to step two. Focus on the good feelings forgiveness can bring you. Remind yourself why you have chosen this path. If you find yourself focusing on the hurt again, loudly say to yourself, 'I choose another thought.' Go for a long walk, talk it through with a friend, read a book on forgiveness. If you keep choosing to move your energy and focus away from the hurt, eventually it will lose its stranglehold.

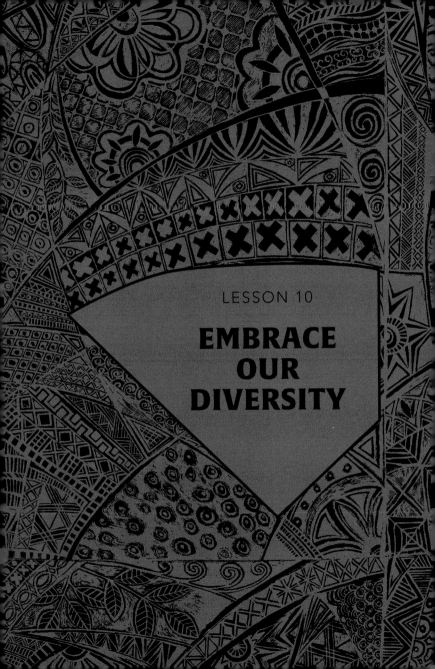

LESSON 10

EMBRACE OUR DIVERSITY

'Knowledge is like a baobab
tree, no one individual's arms
can reach around it.'

African proverb

As human beings, we share our planet with over 8 million different species, but we ourselves are pretty unique. With around 200 countries in the world – official numbers vary – and roughly 6,500 different spoken languages (and with an infinite number of cultural differences), what we all have in common is this: diversity.

However, this diversity strikes fear in many of us. Whether it's food we've never tried before, music we're not used to, or a religious belief we don't understand, sometimes our reaction to things we aren't familiar with or recognize is to turn away. There are even times we actively dislike something simply because it's 'different'. *Ubuntu* tells us to put aside national or societal differences and to see one another for what we are: human beings in this *together*.

At the Desmond Tutu HIV Foundation Youth Centre in South Africa, interns are taught to embrace other cultures rather than to judge them. The centre, run by young people, works with the multicultural community of Masiphumelele, near Cape Town, where people from countries such as Mozambique, Malawi and Nigeria live. As is human nature, it's quite common for young people to find themselves viewing differing cultures with a wary eye, so embracing diversity is actively promoted.

One South African intern, Asisiphe, gave me one simple example: 'Judging is often based around the unknown. For instance, in Zimbabwe and Mozambique they eat very small fish called *matamba*, something we wouldn't consider touching. But actually we learned it is a good source of nutrition and is a readily available food.

Undermining others' cultures serves no purpose, so we're now challenging it when we see it happening.'

Recently, the young interns were also taught about Nigerian music and how Nigerians dance to it using different rhythms. By the end of the session, everyone was happy to try out some new moves, embracing something different rather than reacting in fear and judgement.

FIND EQUALITY IN DIVERSITY

In order to embrace diversity, humility is necessary so we can take time to look for our similarities. Despite being a public figure, my grandfather always made time to chat with the people around him. He always made space so everyone could feel equal, whatever their background. When he made speeches to young people, he often spoke about how even though he might be considered a VIP, he considered them to be VSPs – Very Special Persons. Then he would make the entire audience recite, 'I am a VSP' a few times to really get the point across.

Such a humble attitude helped him in his role as chairman of the Elders too. An international, non-governmental group, the Elders was set up in 2007 from an idea by Richard Branson, Nelson Mandela and Peter Gabriel in which eminent statespersons from around the world gathered to work towards peace.

The first group of Elders was formed with my grandfather as chairman and Nelson Mandela as founder, alongside former US president Jimmy Carter, Graça Machel, Kofi Annan, Mary Robinson, Ela Bhatt, Gro Harlem Brundtland and Muhammad Yunus. The idea was they would meet twice a year to discuss what global causes to focus upon. They

then travelled around the world to talk to people involved in the issues, paying particular attention to the average citizen's points of view before they spoke to leaders.

As my grandfather explained at the inaugural event, 'In traditional society, it was the Elders of the village who were trusted to resolve conflict and provide wise guidance. Today we live in a global village but we do not have our global Elders to lead and inspire.'

To be those Elders was the group's new role.

'We have become not a melting pot but a beautiful mosaic. Different people, different beliefs, different yearnings, different hopes, different dreams.'

Former US president, Jimmy Carter

Instead of all coming from the same place, however, all those involved were from very different backgrounds. Gro Harlem Brundtland was former prime minister of Norway and former director-general of the World Health Organization; Ela Bhatt was an Indian social reformer; Muhammad Yunus was a Bangladeshi economist; and Graça Machel was a Mozambican humanitarian. Such diversity meant each individual brought different skills to the table. Each had their own strengths, but also, perhaps, their own blind spots. In their work together they showed that a group of diverse individuals can go much further and achieve much more than when they all have the same talents.

THE GIFT OF HUMILITY

If we choose to leave our pride and ego at the door and remain humble, embracing other people becomes more joyful and easier.

At the founding event for the Elders, my grandfather spoke about how humbled he felt to be in such great company. 'I am a township urchin. I was born in one of the apartheid locations and sometimes I stand outside of myself and look at me and say, "What? You? From Ventersdorp, hobnobbing with all of these people? It can't be true."'

However, this is what made the group special, and indeed is what can bring any diverse group together. Remaining humble and looking at what others can offer means we can learn from one another, because we see each other as equal beings. Their incredible humility was a key element of the Elders' work, as they were some of the most high-profile and well-respected individuals in the world. Putting their own egos to one side, they chose to focus on others.

Elders in society are not often treated with the respect they deserve. According to the Royal Society for Public Health, in 2018, ageism is rife in Britain. Millennials have the most negative attitudes towards older people, and a quarter of them believe it's normal for older people to be unhappy and depressed. Although there can be a divide between the young and old in political beliefs and ideologies, much wisdom lies with elderly people. Having lived through times younger generations can only imagine, members of the older generations have a wealth of knowledge and experience to draw upon – whoever they are and wherever they're from.

The Elders' decision to undertake a campaign against child marriage and the subsequent creation of the successful organization Girls Not Brides is an example of how much the group has to offer the world. As they enter their second decade of work, they have promoted peace accords in Colombia and Zimbabwe, have travelled extensively to conflict zones and brought hope to the persecuted, and have advocated for universal healthcare as well as calling for action on climate change before it was the 'on trend' thing to do.

THE CONSISTENCY OF BEING HUMAN

If we put aside our judgements of 'the other', we become infinitely stronger. We have to see ourselves as part of a human community, not as separate entities, and our ability to do this is a wonderful part of our human nature. Research even reveals that when we see others being harmed – even complete strangers – the same part of our brain is stimulated as if we were being harmed ourselves. Such findings could go some way to explaining why charitable donations shoot up when a natural disaster unfolds on the news, often regardless of where it's happening in the world. Human beings are designed to care about other people, as *ubuntu* urges.

'**A man bleeds, suffers, despairs not as an American or a Russian or a Chinese, but in his innermost being as a member of a single human race.**'

Adlai Stevenson

So, despite our differences, we are the same. Even if it's the most diverse body of characters that sometimes pushes humanity forward. Civil war almost broke out in Tunisia in 2011 following the Arab Spring of anti-government protests, uprising and rebellion, until a very unlikely alliance, known as the Tunisian Dialogue Quartet, was formed. Four *very* different organizations came together to take up a leadership role and steer the country away from violence and towards peace. They were individuals from the General Labour Union; the Confederation of Industry, Trade and Handicrafts; the Human Rights League; and the Order of Lawyers. Their skillsets brought different talents and their diversity helped to promote peace and compromise in a way the politicians had failed to do. The group even won a Nobel Peace Prize for their efforts. Yes, they were made up of very different members, but they all wanted to strive for the same thing: understanding, unity and – above all – peace in their country.

If we choose to view our diversity as a cause for celebration, and if we extend a hand to people who are not like us, we stand to gain a lot, especially in a global setting. With the internet it's never been easier for people across the world to reach out, join forces and work together, whatever their gender, political conviction or religious belief.

The Global Citizen project is another inspiring endeavour bringing everyone together, regardless of background. It's an initiative founded on the belief that engaged citizens all over the world can bring an end to extreme poverty by 2030 by becoming global thinkers and change-makers, and by using their collective voice. Education and the belief in education to empower lies at the heart of the project. Since 2011, millions of people from countries around the world have taken part in a bid to confront global challenges such as poverty, the environment and women's issues. The project also holds Global Citizen festivals internationally to raise money and awareness, including in South Africa. Recently, the project brought together its biggest group of heads of states and talented artists to celebrate the centenary of Nelson Mandela.

Their clear message is this: it doesn't matter who you are or where you are from, you can join in and make a difference.

EVERYONE BRINGS SOMETHING TO THE TABLE

So how do we learn to embrace our diversity? Especially if somebody else's life is so very different to our own?

Growing up, I saw my own family deal with this challenge and make the choice to embrace *ubuntu*. My grandparents always had an 'open house' and allowed anyone to visit or stay with them if they needed to. The idea was: 'If we have room and people need a place, then they have a place.' So when I went away to school, my mother followed in her parents' footsteps and gave up our spare room for those in need.

A couple of decades ago, while she was giving a presentation at Vanderbilt University in Tennessee about the empowerment of people in the margins, a man named Karl stood up and challenged her about her speech. He asked her why she was giving such a talk in a university that was known to be an institution of great privilege and power. He told her he would have preferred her to speak at one of the historically black universities or colleges (HBCUs) in town, or even a church or community centre.

Karl explained that he himself had experienced homelessness and mental health issues, and knew about life in the margins. After the presentation, he and my mother had a short conversation in which he told her she was part of an elite group that was continuing to have these conversations about marginalized people in inappropriate venues. She explained that she believed these conversations should be had with people in places of comfort and anywhere else people would be happy to go along and listen. She also countered his notion that she was an elite. He replied that he had heard her introduction, and she clarified that while it was her resumé, it was not a full explanation of who she was as a person. At the end of the evening, my mother left, but she still felt judged by Karl.

The following morning Karl got in touch with Mum at her office and told her that he wanted to get to know who she was. From there a friendship developed, and she grew to know him as a decent man with strong ideas, who'd had a tough life and experienced mental illness. When she found out he had recently lost his place to live, she offered him a room for six months.

'Nobody knows everything but everyone knows something.'

African proverb

Ubuntu is never a one-way street. When you show people respect and humanity, and give to them of yourself, they can often reveal a gift to you. In the case of my mother's houseguest, Karl formed an unexpected bond with my brother during his stay. He fulfilled a paternal role in my brother's life for a while and taught him to play chess. Months later, when Karl experienced a mental health crisis for which he needed treatment, it was my brother who insisted he and my mother visit Karl in hospital every day. The relationship had grown into a genuine, supportive friendship on both sides, despite their many differences.

What about the challenges we face when we embrace diversity? How do we overcome the feeling of 'otherness' or concerns we might have about not being able to understand or cooperate with each other? My mother has shown me that you may not know how things will turn out, and you may be learning along the way, but embracing diversity makes the unknown a little more familiar.

DOING THINGS DIFFERENTLY DOESN'T MEAN 'WORSE'

People from the African continent are not known for their good time-keeping. This is a cultural habit, perhaps stemming from not wanting to live their lives by the clock, which Westerners tend to do. However, it can be tricky when everyone is trying to work together.

Eleanor Riley is a charity worker who confronted this challenge when she set up Made With Hope, an organization which helps to alleviate poverty in Tanzania. Her idea was to raise money to build schools and to provide fresh water, sustainable food, energy and education. To kickstart the projects, Eleanor joined forces with a local Tanzanian community organizer, Zuma, who worked with the community on a grassroots level. Eleanor admired Zuma deeply for always keeping his door open to those in need, including the old, sick and mentally unwell. Even in such a poor community, Zuma always had something to give, so she asked him to help her set up Made With Hope.

Only then did Eleanor appreciate the extent of the cultural differences that she would need to find a way to navigate. Zuma and his colleagues didn't understand how fundraising worked in the West, nor did they have any concept of the business strategies or time-keeping Westerners preferred.

So while Zuma taught Eleanor about compassion and what people needed on a grassroots level, Eleanor educated the Tanzanians she was working with about bureaucracy and working set hours for effective fundraising. Eleanor also learned she loved what she called 'African time' as there was no anxiety or rushing around because everyone trusted things would be achieved in the end.

Once we view opposing ways of doing things, or opposing opinions, as something to learn from, we're far more likely to make progress. We don't always have to agree but we can embrace others with different viewpoints to ours.

In our school and work environments in the Western world we are often instructed to focus on what doesn't work rather than what does – we're always looking for mistakes. Children are taught to adhere to a 'one size fits all' approach to learning, and we often view our colleagues' behaviour as right or wrong. *Ubuntu* encourages us to be more open-minded than this. Just because someone does something differently – or not the way we would do it – doesn't mean it's 'wrong'. We're all on our own journey and react individually to situations according to our own life experiences.

Instead of looking at what people aren't bringing to the table, ask yourself what *do* they bring? Maybe the quiet colleague who doesn't speak up at big meetings will have great ideas one-to-one. You simply need to sit down with them in a smaller setting and learn to do things their way. Maybe the very vocal person whose free-flowing ideas you struggle to follow when they're talking might order their thoughts better when they write them down? Being flexible and open-minded brings out the best in people. *Ubuntu* tells us that *every single person* has *something* to offer. We simply need to have more patience or commitment in uncovering it.

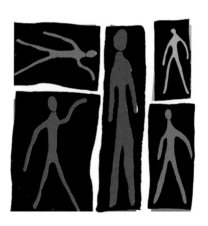

Think about your language. We all have a tendency to stereotype people, according to our experiences and upbringing. Be mindful of the way you speak with bias. Do you often think people from a certain culture are a certain way? If so, challenge this. Be wary if you fall into an 'us' and 'them' way of thinking at work, at school or at home. Think about why this attitude has emerged and consider how you might see things from a different perspective.

Imagine if everyone in the world were the same. It would be a very dull place. Our views, and therefore our progress, would be limited; our experiences would be boring; we would never experience anything new. Yet we often struggle to embrace difference in others. Think of all the myriad things you enjoy from various cultures without even realizing it. It might be the food that you like, the clothes that you wear or the entertainment you enjoy. Everything from Chinese noodles to Malaysian sarongs to Swedish noir films. Then call to mind all the differences within our own families that add to the human experience. You might have a grandparent who loves to cook traditional recipes, a toddler who makes everyone laugh, a moody teenager who shares the latest cultural phenomenon with you. *Everyone has something to offer.*

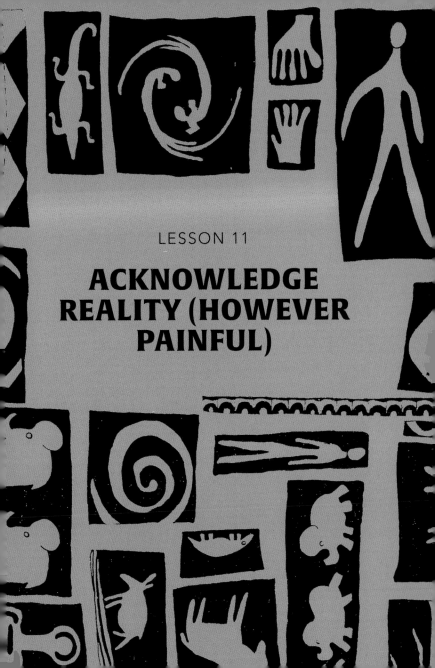

LESSON 11

ACKNOWLEDGE REALITY (HOWEVER PAINFUL)

'Ubuntu is not a biblical concept but an ancient African one. Nevertheless it falls back on one simple thing: that humans have been created for togetherness, and what drives us apart is greed, lust for power and a sense of exclusion, but those are aberrations.'

Allan Boesak

If we want to make progress in life, we first have to accept our current situation. If you deny your reality or refuse to confront the issues that need dealing with, you can often find yourself caught in a loop. Sticking your head in the sand helps nobody, least of all you.

Ubuntu teaches us not to deny our past or our situation, even if it's painful, and tells us that we should accept without blind judgement either what has happened to us or what has happened to other people. It encourages us to embrace all facets of life – the good, the bad and the ugly – and allows us to 'be', accept what's here and now, and to embrace the help of others to work through it.

The aim of the TRC is a good example of how to accept a painful past. The Commission did not flinch from any of the horrors of apartheid. Its legacy was to create a lasting peace in South Africa.

My grandfather said he heard about the worst of humanity at this time. Often, after listening to testimonies, he would weep because the stories were so terrible. He deeply felt the pain of others, such as the mothers of the Gugulethu Seven, who only found out their sons had been murdered when they watched the news on TV.

One of the promises that the TRC tried to uphold was that every murdered son and daughter, parent or loved one would have their remains brought back to their home community to be laid to rest in peace following a proper burial. So taskforces were sent out to look for mass and unmarked graves. This act was about returning dignity to families who had been stripped of it, but it was also about confronting terrible crimes unflinchingly, however awful.

EVERYDAY UBUNTU

One day, a taskforce returned to say they had evidence that some victims had been fed to crocodiles. There were no bodies to be taken home to the families of the murdered. When he received the news, my grandfather broke down and cried, 'But what should we tell the victims' mothers?'

His first thought was for the grieving relatives. During such a devastating time for the bereaved, a sense of *ubuntu* prevailed: empathy for their pain was at the forefront of everyone's minds. Empathy is a product of recognizing reality – yours or someone else's – and the communal outpouring of compassion for the families involved provided some comfort to them.

When we deny the reality of something that has happened, progress towards reparation or resolution is often hindered. If you break your leg, you must deal with the injury and be prepared to wait a while for it to heal. Only then can you walk again. If you try to do so too early, you will only make things worse. Wounds only heal effectively when they are cleaned thoroughly and looked after with care. Otherwise they will fester. The same is true for many real-life situations.

THE REALITY IS: WE *ARE* IN THIS TOGETHER

We *all* face complications in life, feel broken at times, or are unable to deal with it all. And, on occasion, we all struggle to face up to the reality of what is happening to us. Therefore, *ubuntu* teaches us always to look to one another for support.

If you are depressed, it can be painful to analyse why that is. If you hate your job, it can be hard to confront the idea of moving on if you need the money to keep coming in. If you're in a bad relationship, it can be tough to change anything at all unless you're prepared to face the potential fallout, which may include breaking up. Often we just trudge through the day, hoping that tomorrow will be better.

'It rains on every roof.'

African proverb

Ubuntu reassures us that we don't need to struggle alone. To make progress, human beings need other human beings. We need shoulders to cry on and arms to hold us when things go wrong. It's OK to speak out and ask for help. To say we want to change things. To ask other people how they managed in similar situations. We need each other to rely on for support and guidance. When we appreciate this is the reality for everyone, we can grow to understand that there is no shame in reaching out.

We often hide our painful realities because we don't want the outside world to see us as weak or unable to cope – the same goes for other people. Shame struggles to exist if it's got company, though. If you know someone is going through a similar thing to you, it helps hugely to extend a hand to them. Even if you're not going through the exact same thing, when you show empathy you are connecting with the emotions that person may be experiencing, and it will make them feel less alone.

OTHER PEOPLE HELP US FACE OUR REALITY

No one enjoys criticism. Whether it's at work, in our personal life or our own inner voice, criticism is oppressive and unhelpful. It rarely provides any answers but often erodes self-esteem. It can be a way to be heard, but is it the most effective means?

'Find people who will make you better.'

Michelle Obama

If someone makes a harsh comment – something personal or about our work – we'll usually take it to heart. We'll dwell on it. It will gnaw at us. *Was someone right to think that about me? Were they being unfair? Do other people think badly of me?* The voices go round and round in our heads. The criticism isn't justified sometimes, so we'll try to work out if this is the case by asking for other opinions.

Constructive criticism, on the other hand, can be helpful. We need feedback, we crave praise and, at times, can benefit from constructive criticism. Our parents and teachers tell us where we have gone wrong so that we can improve. By their own example they lead the way.

There are times when we don't understand the rules laid out, or don't appreciate the learning when it's taking place. Accepting our parents and teachers know better is something we all need to do. If we are not fortunate enough to trust the people in our lives who are in positions of authority, we can look to trusted friends and other mentors for guidance. *Ubuntu* involves remaining open to learning and changing our behaviour for the greater good of all.

FACING THE OTHER FACES

Confronting reality involves being honest. At times, very honest. It's one of the principles of *ubuntu*. If we cannot be authentic and honest with one another, our relationships are weakened and, ultimately, everyone loses out. The person who is suppressing their true feelings can feel misunderstood or isolated, and people around them can feel confused or ignorant about the reality of their experience.

Joseph Duncan, co-founder of Youth Futures UK and a Tutu Foundation ambassador, says the Ubuntu Round Table was built around people from both sides – those in authority and those who felt challenged by authority – being frank and honest, however uncomfortable the experience became. 'It was a safe place where people could confront their own realities and share them,' he explains.

During one session, the Round Table worked with a group of boys from London who had endured a series of humiliating stop-and-searches by the police. The boys said that the officers would tell them they were looking for drugs or weapons, changing their story and keeping it fluid so the boys felt as if they were being unfairly targeted. However, some boys admitted that, at times, they *were* carrying knives – they felt pressure to do so as others in their community were doing the same thing. On one hand they felt victimized; on the other, they held their hands up to breaking the law.

In turn, the police had to be honest too about their own feelings, including their own prejudices. Many of the officers from the Met had come to work from outside the capital and were white. They hadn't grown up around black communities, and their default was to stereotype the young black men wearing hoodies on a council estate as trouble.

Speaking both their truths was a deeply moving process for the two groups. The pain of what they were really thinking was there to see. However, by being honest about the reality of their everyday lives, and the thoughts running through their minds, something shifted. We saw officers visibly lighten when they heard the other side of the story.

One teenager mentioned his community's belief that the police were rounding up black people merely to hit their arrest targets for the month, a comment which upset the police. 'No wonder you feel you can't trust us if this is what people believe,' one officer said. The police then admitted that they needed to hear more realities from other community members in order to be able to protect them in a meaningful way and do their job properly.

It's human nature to want to shield our eyes from hard realities, and pretend that things are not as bad as they seem. This sometimes feels like the best option. However, if you face up to the worst thing, you then have a chance of finding a solution. *You* get to decide the ending of the story.

My mother grew up hearing her parents speak truthfully throughout her childhood. They warned their children, 'One day we might be arrested or killed for our work.' It was a reality from which my grandparents didn't shy away. They knew the risks of conducting peaceful protests, especially when others were protesting with violence. For them, remaining silent in the face of injustice was worse than being punished for speaking out. At times, it meant my mum and her siblings feared the worst, but they had other family members and friends to rely on. It meant they could accept their unusual lives and, when they were older, understand what service to others means.

My family taught me that *ubuntu* is not about trying to pretend that everything is sweetness and light. It's about understanding that it's possible for us to confront our darkness, especially with the help of others around us, as this makes us human too. Every positive has a negative. And every negative has a positive. To love deeply will involve grief. To stand for a cause, as my grandparents did, will involve sacrifice. To hear constructive criticism can lead to learning. To allow yourself to be vulnerable can ignite compassion and deepen your relationships with those around you.

IT TAKES HUMILITY TO SEE REALITY

A person with *ubuntu* always remains humble. It means putting others first, and being more likely to listen and learn from them. If we see ourselves as less than perfect, we can also accept other people's imperfections and will be less likely to sit in judgement.

'There is a universal respect and even admiration for those who are humble and simple by nature, and who have absolute confidence in all human beings irrespective of their social status.'

Nelson Mandela

My grandfather is always open to others' opinions and having his own convictions challenged, something Mabel van Oranje, who worked with him and the other Elders as their first CEO, told me.

One day, the organization was discussing which global cause to support, when Mabel proposed the idea of helping to end child marriage. It's a worldwide issue, with around one in five girls being forced to marry by the age of eighteen, and Mabel suggested that the Elders might play a catalytic role in addressing this harmful practice. It would make a good campaign for them to get behind.

Initially, my grandfather remained unconvinced. He accepted that it is a terrible social problem but argued that it mainly happened in South Asia and was therefore not a global issue. It was then that Mabel corrected him and revealed that child marriages were common all over the world, with up to 40 per cent of young girls affected in Africa. This fact stunned my grandfather. He was shocked. He had no idea this terrible reality was taking place to such a great extent on his own continent. He admitted he felt ashamed by his ignorance, and went on to state publicly that he would work to end child marriage with the same dedication and determination as he had stood up against apartheid.

The ensuing campaign was a huge success. To that point, child marriage had been a little-known problem, but through the work of the Elders it received worldwide attention and went on to kickstart a new global civil society partnership known as Girls Not Brides. To date, *hundreds of thousands* of girls have been helped to avoid a premature marriage.

Ubuntu teaches us that there is no place for pride when it comes to dealing with each other. We have to support one another and grow together. Everyone gets things wrong sometimes. Everyone feels shame or embarrassment or weakened by a certain incident or situation. It's how we deal with the reality that makes all the difference.

To live authentically we need to be honest with ourselves and others. We need to face our problems head on, and help find solutions with our fellow women and men. In turn, this allows families, communities and societies to move forward together.

Help someone else to face reality. Sometimes it's necessary to confront an individual about their actions. There are kind ways of doing this. If you need to offer constructive criticism in a professional setting, try 'the sandwich method'.

Focus on a positive achievement first, before moving on to the negative things you want to say. Use a straightforward tone but avoid the use of accusatory phrases, such as, 'It was your fault when . . .' Make sure you state facts rather than simply saying what you 'think' or 'feel'. Keep personal emotion out of it when necessary. End with another positive thing about what that person is doing well and then ask if they have any questions. Allow them to respond.

Choose the time and place for this conversation carefully. If you're going to confront a tricky situation – whether it involves a partner, a child or a co-worker – consider where you do it. Face-to-face is always better, as nuances can often be lost in written messages. Try to control your tone of voice – sounding too detached or too abrupt can make people defensive. Always speak to somebody as you would like to be spoken to.

Work on your humility. It's an underrated quality but one from which all of us can benefit. It helps us to listen, to respect others' opinions and to remain open to learning.

It gives us freedom from our own egos too, and having some is more likely to earn you respect. Many of the world's greatest peacemakers put honesty and humility above many other characteristics.

The next time you find yourself in a situation where you feel self-righteous, or are in a rush to criticize, or think that *you* matter the most, consider your humility. Call to mind a person in your life who behaves in a humble manner. How do they conduct themselves? Could you include some of their habits in your own life?

Consider too how good humility feels. If you're not puffed up with pride or focused on putting your needs first, there is an element of freedom to be had.

Acceptance. Many spiritual teachers tell us to focus on the present moment and work on accepting whatever our reality happens to be. This can bring peace of mind, as we stop fighting against what simply 'is'.

Think about what's making you sad, angry or frustrated at the moment. Consider what you can control and what you can't. Remember that worrying is hoping for what you don't want to happen. Concentrate on accepting what you can't change. It's not about giving up, it means you can stop resisting and use your energy for growth in a more positive way.

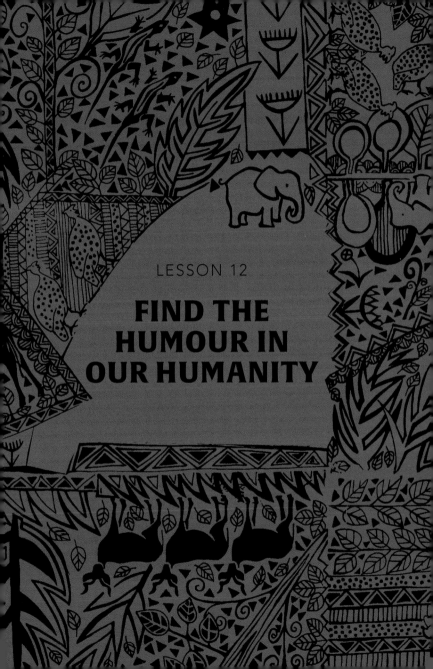

LESSON 12

FIND THE
HUMOUR IN
OUR HUMANITY

'Laughter does wonders
for the heart.'

African proverb

We all love to laugh. It makes us feel better. It's good for our heart health, it reduces stress hormones and boosts feel-good ones, and it also creates bonds. If you make someone laugh, defences are shattered and connections are made. It is the very essence of *ubuntu*.

In our darkest times, sometimes *only* humour can lighten the mood. Humour allows us all to breathe out a little; to change the narrative and the pace of any conversation or situation, especially if it's one of conflict.

In her role as a public speaker, my mother once met Mairead Corrigan Maguire, who was awarded the Nobel Peace Prize in 1976, along with Betty Williams, for their work fighting for peace in Northern Ireland. As part of a group, my mother and Mairead were taking a bus to a peace conference in Colombia, and were upset to find armed guards with automatic weapons on the bus with them.

Sitting in uncomfortable silence, it was hard for the peace activists not to feel disturbed by the armed presence, until Mairead spoke out in a tone filled with amusement: 'Anyone else think it's a little weird we're off to a peace conference guarded by men with automatic weapons?' This little line transformed the atmosphere on the bus instantly from one of tension to one of jollity.

My mother tells me that she sees humour in many of our great leaders. Mairead, as an example, couldn't change the situation she found herself in, but she could encourage others to acknowledge and laugh at it. My mother also tells me that many people filled with *ubuntu* have a 'well of joy' inside themselves. They look and find the light side of life – whatever the circumstances. To see the joy in any moment is a practice we can all learn.

THE LIGHT SIDE OF LIFE

My mother is one of four children. She has two sisters, Thandi and Mpho, and a brother, Trevor. My grandparents were determined their children would have a good education, so my mother and her siblings were sent to boarding school because, at the time, the South African government only provided black children with a Bantu education. This was a racially segregated system involving poorly run schooling and served the interests of white supremacy.

'The laughter of a child is the light of the house.'

African proverb

However, my mother hated her boarding school, as did her older sister, and whenever it was time to say goodbye to their family – at the end of a holiday – they would cry or retreat inside themselves. My grandparents would soon have them laughing again, though. The Tutu family are masters at finding the humour in difficult situations.

My grandmother Leah would make up ridiculous stories about passers-by as they embarked on the long journey to their boarding school, so the girls' tears or silence quickly turned to laughter. She knew their situation couldn't be changed but she wanted to make them feel better. As hard as Leah found the separation from her children, it was the best decision she and my grandfather could make. To ease the suffering, all they could do was find laughter in the moment.

Finding humour in a difficult situation – especially in bleak times when we feel helpless, such as the death of a loved one or the diagnosis of a terminal illness – becomes our last defence. We can lighten the darkness even for a few precious seconds with a wry joke, witty comment or silly thought.

Just like love, a sense of humour is something we can foster. We say, 'see the funny side', because whatever is happening there's *always* a funny side if we look for it. This is especially true when we can't fix a situation or find a solution to a problem. Humour gives us a chance to feel better, despite it all, and it can be a brief reprieve from pain.

WHERE THERE IS NO EXIT, HUMOUR IS A WAY OUT

My grandfather has always been a professional when it comes to breaking the ice with humour. He used to have many jokes up his sleeve for different occasions.

When asked what it took for him to become a Nobel Laureate, he'd say, 'A big nose and sexy legs!' before roaring with laughter at his own joke. My mother tells me how he used to make fun of how ridiculous apartheid was, basing everything on the colour of people's skin. He would say, 'It would be like me deciding I am going to judge people based on the size of their noses. Obviously, since I have a big nose, the big-nosed people would be the better people!'

'Laugh as much as possible, always laugh. It is the sweetest thing one can do for oneself and one's fellow human beings.'

Maya Angelou

My grandfather has never shied away from trying to make people laugh, no matter how tragic the situation. Following the genocide in Rwanda, he visited the region to give a speech to a mixed group of Tutsis and Hutus. These people had been sworn enemies, and everyone in the room had lost many loved ones. For them all to be together, for the first time in a long time, must have been a challenging experience.

My grandfather chose to defuse the tension with a joke everyone could relate to, and told a story about the big-nosed people who excluded a group of small-nosed people. Slowly, the crowd caught on to the fact he was talking about the facial distinctions between Hutus and Tutsis, and the joke broke the tension in the room. Whether you poke fun at yourself or create relatable fun at somebody else's expense, it bursts a bubble. Tension is defused and remains so.

During South Africa's anti-apartheid struggle, my grandfather attended the funerals of many people who had been killed in protests or by the police. Often, these events turned into political rallies with huge tensions engulfing them, especially because big gatherings of any nature were banned. Time and time again, my grandfather made jokes to crowds to help create a bond with the audience before his speech.

'I am asking the government to join the winning side,' is something he would often say. A comical statement, given he was speaking to a people who were living under the burden of repression, and yet still he was calling them the winning side.

He would also joke about race. Once, at a funeral in Johannesburg, he told a joke many might not have dared to deliver; one he has repeated many times since, about God creating human beings. He would explain how God moulded men from clay before placing them in a kiln, as if he were making bricks. He put in the first batch, then became busy with other work and forgot all about what he was making. When he remembered what he was doing, God opened the oven in a panic to find the clay had turned black, and this is how he made black men. When he put in the next batch, he kept checking the time, as he was overly anxious not to overcook them again. On this occasion, he opened the oven too quickly and the second batch came out undercooked. This is how he made white men.

The crowd found this concept very amusing and many people admired his chutzpah at telling a joke about racial division at such an event. His humour put people at ease and gave them a way out of the high tension and emotion of the moment.

THE UNIFYING FORCE OF LAUGHTER

They say laughter is the best medicine, and simply hearing someone laugh can be infectious – no pun intended. Science has shown how important laughter is to our relationships too. One study revealed that humans have evolved to laugh as it sends a 'secure, safe message to others'. After all, it's possible to fake a smile, while laughter is more involuntary and therefore authentic. If someone is laughing you are less likely to view them as a threat.

With authenticity at its heart, humour can be used to inspire and lead others. During his role as chairman of the Elders, my grandfather put humour to good use during challenging times while chairing meetings. The group he was working with was like no other. It included former presidents, human rights campaigners and peace activists. These people were among the most prominent and well-respected individuals in the world. So how does one even try to manage such a gathering?

For most people it would have been an intimidating experience, but my grandfather always used humour to get his point across. If a former president walked in late, he would ask them loudly, 'Do we need to buy you a watch?' Or, if someone interrupted a fellow speaker, he would play on his belief in God. 'Do you want to go to the hotter place later on?' he'd chide. Equally, if someone deserved serious praise, he would respond, 'I may recommend you for a place in heaven.'

Humour can make us laugh at ourselves as well as with others. It's the ultimate leveller. If we are in a room and all of us laugh together at the same thing, we experience a precious moment of happiness together, regardless of who we are.

Africa has a long history of using humour to defuse tensions, as is seen in its proverbs.

'The monkey who tries to see the hunter clearly collects bullets in its eyes.'

Congolese proverb

'However much the buttocks hurry, they will always remain behind.'

Cameroonian proverb

'He who thinks he is leading and has no one following is only taking a walk.'

Malawian proverb

HUMOUR TO SAVE THE DAY

Poet Dumi Senda, who now also works as a global diversity coach and consultant, tells the story of how he once used humour to defuse a potentially volatile situation at a peace conference in Sarajevo to which he'd been invited to speak and share his poetry. He had been warned by contemporaries to be mindful of walking around alone in the city, as very few ethnic minorities live in the region. A black face might attract unwanted attention, he was told.

After a successful conference, Dumi embraced the spirit of *ubuntu* and went for a wander into the nearby town. Almost instantly he found himself attracting attention. He couldn't walk a few metres without someone asking for a selfie, with many locals declaring openly that they'd never seen a black person before. He was even mistaken for Jay Z, which made him laugh.

Before long, a crowd gathered and began to ask him questions: 'Is it true Africans live in trees?' 'Is it true Africans walk around naked?' Dumi's natural reaction was to feel offended. Were these people being racist? Were they ignorant? He chose to swallow his defensive response and flip the impending tension through the use of humour.

'Yes,' he replied, laughing. 'Africans sometimes live in trees, just like some Europeans live in tree houses.' He also joked that Africans do walk around naked . . . in the shower, as do Europeans.

The crowd quickly understood that his jokes were at their expense and they broke into laughter. They acknowledged that they'd been drawn into holding incorrect, stereotypical views of black Africans and Dumi accepted a drink from them in a local bar. What could have become an angry standoff turned into genuine camaraderie.

We can cry. We can rage. We can sink into a depression. But, sometimes, laughing in the face of a difficult situation is the best antidote. Laughter gives us back control, however briefly. It brings respite and, at times, relief. Humour also allows us to show our humanity, because it's an attractive quality that lifts all our spirits. We gravitate towards people who make us laugh for good reason.

Turn a situation around by finding the funny side. Think of a time when something really embarrassing happened to you. Then re-tell the story to someone you know – choose that friend with a contagious laugh (we all have one) – as if it's nothing more than an amusing anecdote. That's when the funny side of your experience should reveal itself. Use this reflection whenever something irritating or out of the ordinary happens, when you've faced something that has thrown you. It could be when something you own breaks unexpectedly, or when you find yourself in a situation that's out of your control or has majorly inconvenienced you. Little things sent to try us can often elicit a laugh. Choose to laugh when you can.

Learn to laugh at yourself. Self-acceptance is key when it comes to being able to do this. If you take yourself too seriously nothing seems funny, but if you learn to view yourself and others in a light-hearted way, humour often follows. We will all go through many similar experiences during our lifetime. Identifying our own humanity and sharing it with others is what *ubuntu* is all about. Having a sense of humour helps us to live longer too – a seven-year study carried out in Norway revealed it increases the probability of living into retirement. Laughter is, quite literally, a lifesaver.

Seek out humour. Whether it's watching more comedy on TV, going to a stand-up gig, or hanging out with witty friends, exposing ourselves to humour helps us to see the funny side of life more often. This exposure is especially important if we don't come from a family where there's a lot of humour. It's possible to develop the ability to laugh more freely, and we should try to do so whenever we can. The more we try, the easier it becomes – and the more joy it brings.

LESSON 13

WHY LITTLE THINGS MAKE A BIG DIFFERENCE

'If you think you're too
small to make a difference,
you haven't spent the
night with a mosquito.'

African proverb

'Be the change you wish to see in the world' is a quote that is often attributed to Mahatma Gandhi. An inspiring concept, but how often have you felt that whatever you do, it won't make a difference? At least, not one that _really_ matters.

Will recycling one piece of rubbish have that much of an impact when you see so much other litter strewn in the street? Will showing up at a popular event really matter if, on the day, you can't be bothered? How about turning out to vote? Someone else will do it, right? Sometimes it's easy to think our input won't have any bearing on a situation, but such an outlook can lead us to feel pointless and lost. After all, if we don't believe our actions will make a difference, it's hard to have faith in the bigger picture.

When it comes to _ubuntu_, we _all_ count and so does everything we do. Every single tiny act can snowball into something bigger. Even if it doesn't appear to make an impact immediately, it's the possibility that it can that makes it worth it. You never know what might happen until you try.

ALL OF US MATTER, INCLUDING *YOU*

When Mother Teresa left her convent to go and work alongside the poorest people of Calcutta (now Kolkata), she had no idea what would happen next. She was just one person trying to help. Decades later it led to her being awarded the Nobel Peace Prize. 'We ourselves feel that what we are doing is just a drop in the ocean,' she said. 'But the ocean would be less because of that missing drop.'

We don't all have to be Nobel Peace Prize winners to feel as if what we do makes a difference. Every chance encounter, every interaction, every effort we make has the capacity for the greater good and enrichment of our own lives.

Take the One Billion Acts of Peace campaign, which was set up by the PeaceJam Foundation in partnership with fourteen Nobel Peace laureates, including my grandfather, to encourage thoughtful actions aimed at creating world peace. PeaceJam founders Dawn Engle and Ivan Suvanjieff, who began the movement after years of watching the impact the youth and Nobel Peace laureates were having in their communities, say they're convinced big problems in the world can be tackled by ordinary people. 'Everyone matters. Everyone can make a difference,' they say.

They chose ten areas to focus on, including poverty, helping women and children, the environment, and ending race and hate. The campaign encourages us to start from something as simple as making lunch for a homeless person, picking up litter in the community or participating in an event from a different culture. These little decisions to take part and join in can lead to something bigger for everyone.

Often we have nothing to lose by trying. We can find inspiration, new friends and connections by getting out into the world and holding on to the intention of making it a better place.

'A mountain is composed of tiny grains of earth. The ocean is made up of tiny drops of water. Even so, life is but an endless series of little details, actions, speeches, and thoughts. And the consequences whether good or bad of even the least of them are far-reaching.'

Swami Sivananda

TINY ACTS *CAN* CHANGE NARRATIVES

When my grandfather was a small boy, he lived in a poor black township in Sophiatown. One day, he met the white priest Trevor Huddleston, who was a champion for the dispossessed in South Africa and would do anything for anyone, regardless of their colour. Huddleston passed my grandfather and his mother on the street, and raised his hat to my great-grandmother in respect. This tiny act took seconds, but meant the world to my grandfather. A white man had shown his mother, a black woman, respect. This had never happened before and this small gesture made him view white people differently.

Father Trevor, as my grandfather called him, got to know my grandfather and went to visit him while he lay in hospital with tuberculosis as a young boy. His gentle, caring manner made him very popular with all the kids, but for my grandfather it was proof that not all white people treated black people with disrespect

Decades later, when she was a little girl, Ingrid von Stein met my grandfather for the first time in a church where he was preaching. This time, *he* was one of the first black people *she* had ever met. Ingrid had grown up with only poor views of black people – and, indeed, men in general, as her father was abusive.

When my grandfather smiled at her, warmly asking her how she was, Ingrid was bowled over. He then went on to deliver a sermon with his trademark humour, making everyone laugh. Later, they got chatting and Ingrid felt that he listened to her in a way no other man had ever done. To my grandfather, it was just another day in church, just another conversation with a human being, but the warmth he showed this little girl made a profound difference. Unbeknown to both of them at the time, one day Ingrid would go on to work for him.

These small, seemingly insignificant moments are catalysts for change. We can't always expect big things to come from small things, but a simple act of yours can mean something important to someone else. A generous smile. Asking 'How are you?' with genuine sincerity. A kind offer to do a small deed. They all add up. Especially to those who least expect it.

TEAMWORK WITH STRANGERS

In 1999, BBC correspondent David Harrison made a *Panorama* programme about a woman called Cynthia Mthebe, a widow with four children who lived in poverty in the Tembisa township north of Johannesburg.

The BBC filmed Cynthia with her friends, scratching around for a living, collecting tins from the local rubbish dump and surviving in a tiny shack in a violent township. This devoted mother did her utmost to keep her place clean and always got her children to school. In the film, she spoke with genuine warmth about wanting to improve her life.

When the programme was aired, the response from viewers was overwhelming. People simply loved Cynthia's positive view of the world, despite her clear hardship. This was before the age of social media, so no one viewer knew what others were thinking or doing, but individually they decided to donate cash.

Money poured into the BBC offices, and funds were passed on to Cynthia. Such was the goodwill of the people, enough money was collected to build her a new house in a better part of town. Later, she gave the house to her children, and one of them went on to achieve his dream of becoming a DJ.

These huge changes to Cynthia's life and those of her children all stemmed from people sitting at home in a country far away, moved en masse by the plight of a stranger. It's not just money we can give, though. It can be our time. It can be whatever else we have to hand – sometimes we need only to look around us to see what resources we have available, however small they seem to be.

In a small village in Rwanda, with the help of the charity Tearfund, a mother called Claire took part in training about harnessing local resources. She then used her initiative to set up a sewing cooperative from very humble beginnings. First of all, tailors in the area were asked for leftover materials and ends of spools, which were then cut into patchwork. Then, Claire and a friend, despite having little sewing experience, made items that were good enough to sell.

At first, there was only one sewing machine, but as money came in from sold goods, they were able to teach other ladies how to sew. Gradually, the pool of tailors supplying them with unwanted scraps of material grew. Within a year, the Urukundo Sewing Cooperative was well under way. Since 2013, they have gone from strength to strength, expanding from one machine to nine, including an electric one.

The co-op has had a big effect on Claire's life. Her husband, a long-distance truck driver, was able to give up a job that took him away from his family when he learned to sew himself. What started with just a few scraps of donated cloth is now a thriving livelihood. From something small grew something life-changing.

THE BIGGEST GIFT YOU CAN GIVE IS YOUR TIME

Time is a precious gift because once it's gone, it's lost for ever. Spending your time wisely feels good; wasting it feels pointless. Serving others, *ubuntu* tells us, is never wasted time.

'Time is a teacher.'

African proverb

At Christmas 2018, it made the news that charities such as Shelter, who run soup kitchens and Christmas dinner events for the homeless, are overwhelmed by volunteers during the festive period. The 2018 UK Giving report revealed that charities receive the greatest number of financial donations in November and December. In the US, nearly one-third of annual giving occurs in December, according to NeonCRM, a non-profit software solution company that works with charities. However, during the rest of the year, many charities struggle to achieve the same levels of donations and help.

Volunteering time or giving money needn't be confined to once a year. All-year-round places such as food banks or women's refuges urgently need our support. Donations of a few extra tins of food or a bag of unwanted clothes go a long way, especially if many of us join in. It may feel that individually you're giving very little, but collectively we're able to give a lot.

With the best will in the world, it sometimes isn't possible to give our time. We can easily get caught up in the work/sleep cycle and rarely take time for anything, even ourselves. If giving money or time is not an option, there are other ways of spreading *ubuntu* in the world, including really simple things that cost us nothing – smiling, for instance.

There is genuine power in a smile. Researchers from Uppsala University, Sweden revealed in a study that seeing other people smile suppresses the control we have over our own smiles, making us want to return one. Evolution has made smiling contagious. We feel better when we smile, as it boosts levels of the feel-good hormone serotonin, and so our smile can end up making others feel better too.

A smile says so much: *I am your friend, I am approachable, do not fear, I am reaching out to you.* It's a physical expression of *ubuntu*. Even for those to whom we cannot give our money or time, we can spread a sign of friendship and love in the time it takes to smile. Even if it's one for a passing elderly lonely neighbour on the street or the cleaner in the corridor at work. Making small efforts to show we care is what everyone is looking for.

THE LANGUAGE OF *UBUNTU*

Small acts of kindness in our everyday lives are another way to spread the message of *ubuntu* in the world. There are millions of means of sharing this gift. Tiny acts create good feelings in our communities, such as bringing your work colleague a coffee in the morning without them asking, offering your seat to an elderly or pregnant passenger on the train, passing along a book you enjoyed to someone else, clearing your table in the café when you've finished. The list is endless.

Ubuntu is about gently putting other people's needs first. Without fanfare or expecting anything in return, we see other people before we see ourselves – or as ourselves – so we treat them the same. Giving away more than we take, putting someone ahead of us.

These tiny acts are not completely altruistic – you will gain from them too. Who doesn't get a kick out of being thanked with sincerity, or if someone is surprised and delighted by the little thoughtful thing you did? The other person feels nurtured and you light up inside. And you carry that light with you into the world.

We live in an age of self-absorption, self-development and self-obsession. We live in the age of the selfie! Unfortunately, studies show that thinking of 'I' all the time is actually a sign of distress. Researchers in Germany, headed by Johannes Zimmermann, found those who answered questions in their study using first-person singular pronouns showed more signs of mental health problems, such as anxiety or eating disorders, than those who did not use them with such regularity.

If we see the world only from our own eyes and put 'I' first every time, a sense of peace and contentment will elude us. Try focusing on other people rather than yourself in conversations and in your thought processes. It shifts anxiety and makes us more self-aware and loving. We'll feel better for implementing *ubuntu* in our everyday interactions. Language might seem like a 'little thing' but the way we use it makes a big difference.

Speaking up for others who cannot easily speak up for themselves (such as the young or the persecuted), turning a conversation towards the person with whom we're speaking and asking questions in a genuinely authentic manner are all small ways in which we can show *ubuntu* in our exchanges.

These days, it's easy for things to get lost in translation via text or email. 'Say it, forget it; write it, regret it' is one saying I stand by. You can always explain yourself and your point of view far better face-to-face. Although it's nice to think we're only responsible for what we say – not how people interpret it – that isn't the reality of human interaction. It's difficult to forget a misread text, or an email that didn't translate well.

Yes, it might be quicker or easier to jot down a message, but the importance of taking time for human interactions shouldn't be underestimated. When we have dealings with someone in person, there are all sorts of non-verbal signals, such as body language and emotion, which we pick up on. Stronger bonds are more likely to form, whether it's for work or pleasure. A quick lunch, coffee or drink after work might seem insignificant, but it can help build connections and friendships we might not otherwise have enjoyed.

SEEKING OUT THOSE LITTLE THINGS IS A BIG THING

It's often the small things in life that give humans the greatest pleasure. A hug from a loved one when you need it, a good chat with a friend when you lose all track of time, a delicious home-cooked meal when you're ravenous, or even a cold glass of water when you're thirsty.

Consciously seeking out joy in such moments makes them easier to spot and appreciate when they arise. When Nelson Mandela left prison, he was so grateful for simplicity. 'After one has been in prison,' he said, 'it is the small things that one appreciates; being able to take a walk whenever one wants, going into a shop and buying a newspaper, speaking or choosing to remain silent. The simple act to control one's person.'

This basic gratitude goes a long way to helping us find contentment. This includes being grateful for our health, our loved ones and having 'enough' – whether it's a roof over our heads, sufficient food, freedom or friends. Being grateful for the small things is vital, for when we recognize how much we have, we can then see that those things add up to something big: a good life.

Ubuntu tells us that gratitude for other people and what they do for us is what makes us human. Whether it's our partner, our children, our classmates, our work colleagues, the bus driver who gets us home or the chef who prepares our takeaway. There's a whole network of people busy helping us, doing small things for us, often without us acknowledging their deeds. All of this adds up to a great sense of *ubuntu* in our lives.

We can choose to be a person who helps, aids, assists and makes a difference. Or we can choose to hide away and take whatever we can get. One choice will lead us to a life of contentment; the other will leave us feeling empty and as if we never have 'enough'. If we make a conscious effort for *ubuntu* to be part of our human experience, we will find what we're looking for as well as spreading more joy in our world.

Every drop makes a difference, so decide today where your drop will land.

Showing up matters. Often, at the end of a long day, we don't feel like going out, doing that good turn we promised to do, or making that phone call we said we would make. However, if we try, we very often will reap the rewards of our actions. No matter how tired you are, always make the effort to do the things to which you've committed. Otherwise you'll feel disappointed in yourself. We don't need to set tasks every day which will change the world or result in huge achievements. Small hurdles and little challenges all add up to something significant and often give the most pleasure.

Whatever we *give* we *receive*. If you think something is missing in your life, then give that particular thing to someone else. For example, if you want more friends, be a better friend to the people you know. If you don't feel listened to, try listening to someone else. If you want more love in your life, give love to others. An act of kindness will inevitably return to you, often in ways you least expect.

Think about the small things that make a difference. Our impact on the environment is a good example. We can't all be environmental activists, dedicating our lives to the cause, running campaigns and attending demonstrations, but we can all choose to recycle and stop wasting water, or cut down on meat and avoid taking unnecessary flights. If *everyone* does these little things it will lead to great change.

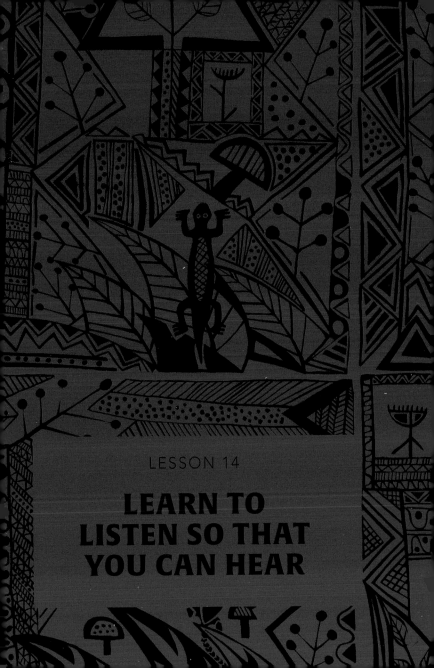

LESSON 14

LEARN TO
LISTEN SO THAT
YOU CAN HEAR

'Much silence makes a
powerful noise.'

African proverb

'Ears that do not listen
accompany the head when
it is chopped off.'

African proverb

It's easy to think that listening is a simple thing to do. Every day most of us will have a conversation, even if it's just the polite chit-chat of asking, 'How's things?' But how often do we make a conscious effort to really _hear_ the answer?

There's a big difference between passive and active listening. We might say, 'I didn't hear that,' when what we really mean is, 'I didn't understand or empathize with what was said.' Imagine someone tells you and a friend a story and, later on, you discuss that same story with your friend. You both might remember it completely differently. You might not have heard what your friend did, because we see the world as we are and often hear it as we are too.

When we do feel a connection or empathy, we say, 'I hear you!' because we have listened and understood. It feels good for both the listener and the speaker. We see our own humanity in one another, we feel less alone and our human experience becomes richer.

Passive listening is the way most of us listen most of the time and it often happens when we're distracted. If the person speaking to us is slow to talk or hesitant, we might feel impatient for them to finish. We focus on this emotion more than what they're actually saying. We might jump in and interrupt, or we might start to rehearse in our minds what we're going to say next. By the time the other person has finished speaking, we've often heard only what we want to hear.

When we listen actively, we give the person to whom we're speaking our full attention. We are mindful to maintain good eye contact, we'll wait for the other person to finish, we'll block out distractions around us and we won't have our response ready for the second they're done speaking. When we listen properly we notice body language, and what non-verbal cues might be trying to tell us. If someone has their arms folded when they're speaking to us, they might be feeling defensive. If they're unable to look us in the eye, they might be feeling uncomfortable. If we don't understand something, we'll ask for clarification.

The young interns who work alongside the local community in the Desmond Tutu HIV Foundation Youth Centre in South Africa work on their active listening skills when dealing with local school kids. One intern, Lazola, explains the importance of such a skill in helping those who have grown up in poverty and might not have the opportunities to express themselves in school or at home.

'We sit and listen to the kids without interrupting, without lecturing or telling them what to do,' he says. '[At the centre], they are allowed space to voice exactly what is on their minds, and only when they've finished do we offer to help, if they ask for it. The importance of being heard should never be underestimated.'

In order for people to be heard, we must first know how to listen. Active or 'deep' listening involves empathy, and this can bring a sense of relief to the speaker. Everyone can tell the difference between being listened to and being heard. We cannot make progress if we refuse to listen to people we don't necessarily agree with. *Ubuntu* invites us to listen to others as we would like to be heard.

HEARING IN ACTION

The Tutu Foundation's Ubuntu Round Table is based upon the skills of deep listening. During one of our sessions in London, a young teenager arrived at the table in a state of upset. Her younger brother had been taken away by social services and the girl, aged just fourteen, hadn't been told why. All she felt was the pain of her sibling's absence. She wanted answers from those in authority.

'I learned to have the patience to listen when people put forward their views, even if I think those views are wrong. You can't reach a decision in a dispute unless you listen to both sides.'

Nelson Mandela

Before the police and social services involved spoke to her at the Round Table, they simply sat and listened, without trying to interrupt. The girl poured out her upset and confusion about the situation. By the time she had finished, everyone in the room was deeply moved.

Only after she'd finished did the policeman involved in the case speak. He explained gently the circumstances leading up to the decision to remove her brother. The issue was one of safeguarding and the decision had been taken as a last resort.

It had been in the best interests of the girl's brother at the time, but she would be able to arrange visits with him. The way in which the police and social services spoke to this upset young woman, as they answered her questions with patience, engaged her. By the time they'd finished, she fully understood the situation and realized they were on her side as much as possible. She still didn't agree with their actions but could appreciate why they'd made the call. By the end of the session the police and the team from social services were far more empathetic about the knock-on effects of their work, and the girl felt heard for the first time.

The Tutu Foundation has also been involved in helping people who work for the NHS overcome difficult situations in the workplace. Healthcare is an emotive subject for lots of people, as we're at our most vulnerable when we need medical treatment, and with the added pressure of services under strain, in life-or-death situations, it can be a pressure-cooker environment to work in.

One case study that helped to train Tutu facilitators to improve their listening skills involved heartbroken families. One particular couple were parents to a son who had suffered a severe asthma attack and had been taken for treatment in A&E. However, during the course of his visit there, a nurse was distracted by another emergency and, because of faulty equipment, the child didn't get the oxygen he needed. Tragically, this lack of oxygen resulted in brain damage.

Absolutely devastated, the angry parents brought a lawsuit against the NHS. The parents' main motivation in bringing the case was so that other parents never had to endure the pain they were facing.

As conversations continued, it came to light that any payout awarded to the family would impede the planned replacement of outdated equipment in the hospital's children's ward. The parents then realized that winning their lawsuit would negatively impact their main aim of preventing another child suffering the same fate as their son.

The NHS Trust listened and heard the parents' concerns, and vice versa. Putting their raw emotion aside, the brave parents came to the conclusion that they wanted the money to be used for the ward. In turn, the NHS Trust allowed the parents to visit the hospital and see the improvements as they were implemented. The outcome for both parties was the best it could be in such tragic circumstances, and the story goes to show how important it is to listen to both sides of an argument.

Often, in situations such as this, emotion can leap in before logic. The late Paul Randolph, a mediator and expert advisor to the Tutu Foundation, referred to it as the 'amygdala hijack', where our fight-or-flight response is activated. The parents had every right to feel let down and furious, but each side came to appreciate the other's point of view to reach this outcome, and that could only be achieved by listening actively.

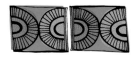

WHAT WILL YOU HEAR IF YOU LISTEN?

By listening or hearing without judgement, we can make progress towards living better, even if we're deeply hurt or upset. When the Elders was first formed, the organization said that listening should be the number-one priority. Since they began their work, they have travelled all around the world, listening to people's stories and the issues that concern them. In each situation, they insist on hearing the viewpoints of people on the street first, before those of leaders and dignitaries. After all, if they don't know what ordinary people are thinking, how can they be advocates for the change people actually want to see?

When we actively listen to what someone else is saying but do not agree with them, it can be a challenge. The Buddhist monk and peace activist Thich Nhat Hanh makes the point that if we react with anger, nothing good will come of it. If we listen and find our compassion, however, then we can act from a place of better energy. If we ask people enough questions and practise 'deep listening', he says we can prevent conflict – and even war.

He also advises that we ask this of others: 'Please tell us about your suffering, your difficulties, I am eager to learn and understand.'

The TRC demonstrated their capacity for deep listening when they received the testimony of individuals involved in crimes during apartheid, and there were many famous cases. For my mother, one of the most powerful testimonies she heard wasn't from anyone who appeared at the Commission, but from someone who had written a letter after listening to the early sessions. He was a young white man and his letter was then read at a hearing in Cape Town.

'In his letter,' she told me, 'he spoke about not knowing about all the atrocities that happened during apartheid. He did not know about the deaths in police custody, the forced removals of whole communities and the awfulness of the Bantu education, and so on. Then he apologized because he realized he'd chosen not to know. He spoke about choosing not to listen and thanked the TRC for making him listen.'

Think of all the times you've chosen not to listen. We all do it. Sometimes, we turn away from someone when they are trying to tell us something, because it's inconvenient, or because we don't believe we have the time. It could be something seemingly small – such as feeling too busy to pay attention to what our child is saying – or huge – such as ignoring the news about devastating effects of global warming.

Ubuntu is about making a pact to listen more, even when we think it doesn't affect us in the here and now. Think of the impact it has on others and the knock-on effect on the world in which we live. There's a satisfaction in taking the time to listen. We will gain knowledge and empathy, and feel more connected to the person who is speaking.

SPREAD THE RELIEF OF BEING HEARD

The relief someone experiences when they have been heard is immense, but the pain of not being heard is all around us. Mental health issues, suicide and self-harm – all these stem from people carrying the burden of pain which isn't expressed, often because it doesn't feel safe to do so, or because it feels as if no one is listening.

The Samaritans bases its life-saving charitable work on the power of listening. It operates a twenty-four-seven, all-year-round telephone service for people who need to talk. It was formed in 1953 by an English vicar who encouraged his local community to volunteer to listen to people who felt suicidal. This was after he lost a fourteen-year-old female member of his congregation to suicide. She feared she had an STD when actually she'd just started her period.

Today, the Samaritans run a campaign called SHUSH, which stands for:

Show you care
Have patience
Use open questions
Say it back
Have courage to help people understand the art of listening

An ability to listen lies at the heart of *ubuntu*. It's about giving time and attention to others, allowing them to feel heard and know they matter. To listen with humility and an open heart is all that's required to enable us to live better, together.

Think of a time when you haven't felt heard. It's happened to all of us. Be it in school, at work, or in a family situation, there will have been occasions when we have desperately wanted our point of view to be appreciated but it has fallen on deaf ears. Try to remember how this emotion felt the next time you're too busy to listen to someone who also needs to feel heard.

Take a little time to check what someone means. Our life's view is clouded by our own experience, which can lead to prejudice. If someone opens up to you and you immediately find yourself thinking, 'Ah yes, I know exactly what they mean!', take a few moments to double-check whether you actually do. You could try summarizing what they've said and repeating it back to them, or ask them outright. 'Let me just check. Is what you're saying . . . ?' This will give the person to whom you're speaking the opportunity to be understood completely and you won't be projecting your own experience on to them.

Not everyone is in a good place to listen. Sometimes we have to accept this. It's a harsh reality but occasionally we have to walk away from someone with whom we're trying to communicate. It could be an embittered ex-partner, a friend who is full of anger or a disgruntled work colleague. Occasionally, it doesn't matter how good our intentions are or how clearly we're trying to communicate, we must accept it's not the time or the place. We can always try again.

EPILOGUE

BRINGING *UBUNTU* INTO YOUR LIFE: 14 LESSONS FROM THE RAINBOW NATION

1. **See yourself in other people.** Open your eyes and look into those of your fellow human beings. We can recognize ourselves in everyone around us if we try to find the connection. There is one, especially where you least expect it.

2. **Strength lies in unity.** We all have wants and desires, but the most likely way of reaching our destination or goal is to join forces with those around us. There is help out there if you look for it. There are people out there with the same ideals as you. When we isolate ourselves we go against our nature, as humans are naturally meant to live together. Explore how others can help you and you'll definitely be pleasantly surprised.

3. **Put yourself in the shoes of others.** Talk to the people with whom you disagree. Imagine for a moment why they think like they do. Consider what events might have led a person to having a different viewpoint to your own. These are things we can all do to try to see life from another person's perspective. Slipping our feet into someone else's shoes can be an uncomfortable or inspiring experience – either way, we can all gain from it.

4. **Choose to see the wider perspective.** It is an absolute choice to decide to explore the bigger picture of what is happening in your life or the world around you. Open your mind and enquire about every angle. Seek out truth and understanding rather than deciding 'my way or the highway!' A limited view of events isolates us and keeps us small- and narrow-minded. Appreciate that almost nothing in life is black or white, but most often is a shade of grey. There is no need to feel you must own a definite opinion on any given subject. You can keep an open mind and change it as you grow. Ignorance is not bliss in the long term; ask the questions you are curious about. Accepting the complexities makes us more compassionate people.

5. **Have dignity and respect for yourself and others.** Having respect for oneself is an inside job and something to nurture. Do at least one or two things each day to make yourself feel good. It could be exercise, seeing a friend, meditation or eating at least one good meal. Your mind and body are equally important. Then decide to afford others the same respect. If we refuse to show others dignity we take it away from ourselves too.

6. **Believe in the good of everyone.** If you look for the good in someone you *will* find it, and inspire and encourage others to feel good about themselves. If you look to criticize, you will find something you don't like. By spotting the good in someone, we boost the self-belief of others and will see more of it. Human beings might be complicated, but by far the majority

of us *are good people*. None of us is born knowing how to hate; we are only taught how to do so by others. Look around you today and decide to spot the good in people, in every single individual you encounter. Notice how good this makes you feel, and how their goodness becomes easier to spot the more you look.

7. **Choose hope over optimism.** A hopeful nature is not a stupid or naive one. It's a wonderful gift for yourself and others. *Ubuntu* shows us we all need hope in our lives, so spread it from your own life outwards. Choose to hope for the positive outcome in *any* given situation. When a sense of hopelessness strikes (and it does to us all at times!) recognize when it's happening and allow yourself time to refocus. Explore what gives you faith in everyday life. This could be healthy eating, relying on good friendships for advice, the foundation of family, a religious or spiritual belief . . . Whatever it is, nurture what gives you the flame of hope in life and fan those flames!

8. **Seek out ways to connect.** It doesn't matter if you're an introvert or an extrovert, human beings are designed to thrive together. Strong relationships will give us more pleasure than any amount of money or number of material things ever could. Every day look for what helps connect you to other people, even if you find yourself physically alone for whatever reason. Disconnection drives sadness. The more connected you feel to others, the happier you will be. It's worth the effort and time to reach out, for all our sakes.

9. **The power of the F-word – forgiveness.** There is something or someone we all harbour a grudge against, either openly or secretly. Think about what this is for you and how you might finally let it go. Forgiving is about relieving the burden on ourselves and other people. When whole nations forgive, wars are prevented. When families forgive, bonds can be restored. When you forgive, you will feel the warmth in your belly. Let's bring the power of forgiveness out into the open and breathe a collective sigh of relief when we feel the pain of the past melt away. If you choose to forgive, your life will blossom and a burden *will* be lifted – a wonderful feeling that's guaranteed.

10. **Embrace our diversity.** As a species, human beings have one thing in common – our differences. It's what has propelled us forward but also what threatens to hold us back. Look around you today and see how many cultures, talents, opinions and experiences help shape our world. Then, imagine if everything was uniform and without this colour. Let's draw on the strengths of our differences and leave the judgement behind.

11. **Acknowledge reality.** If we don't accept the truth of where we are, we won't be able to navigate to where we want to be. Fully accepting and even embracing what is happening today can help us change tomorrow for the better. If we ignore or try to brush realities under the carpet, they never go away. Today, be honest about where you are and where you would like to be. Look to others for inspiration for your journey. Speak your truth about your reality to others and see how they can help.

12. **Find humour in our humanity.** There is no better way to feel *ubuntu* in our lives than through the power of laughter. Spotting the humour in a situation is a precious gift, one we should encourage every day. Humour is an attitude to make life more fun, more inviting and more attractive to ourselves and other people. Being able to laugh during the worst of times lifts our spirits immediately like nothing else. Learning to laugh in the face of the difficulties we all experience is a secret strength of every human being.

13. **Why little things make a big difference.** It's easy to think the smallest of actions don't have consequences, and very occasionally they don't . . . But more often, they do. Take heart that *you* matter, and the way you choose to live does too. Especially when it comes to the environment and our personal conduct, every little act adds up. Also, when we behave well, do a good turn or know we are making a positive difference, we inspire others and feel so much better about ourselves. From choosing to use a reusable water bottle to buying sustainable meat to picking up our litter, there are *thousands* of little things we can do to instantly make the world a better place for all.

14. **Learn to listen so that you can hear.** When it comes to *ubuntu*, good communication is the basis of making the strong connections we all need. Everyone we meet likes and appreciates being heard, so let's start trying to actively listen today. We can learn more, feel more compassion, will be less likely to judge, and will grow as human beings if we can only learn to truly hear what is being said. Every conversation we have can tell us more if we choose to listen deeply. Opening minds, hearts and ears helps us to see others in ourselves.

We can all agree that humans are complex – as is life! But *ubuntu* does not ask that you ignore the complexities of the individual situations in which you find yourself, but that you apply it as best you can.

With *ubuntu* in our world, every day is a new day and a new start.

Progress is not always linear and we will fail on some days, but we can all overcome the pain of our failures. It is the pain of our regrets that sits with us, because it will mean that we didn't do our best or give all that we could. If you practice self-compassion, it will be much easier to practise incorporating *ubuntu* into your life.

Everyday Ubuntu was a joy to write and only made possible thanks to so many inspiring people sharing their stories with me. May *ubuntu* bring as much purpose and satisfaction into your own life as it has into mine. And may you see yourself in the people in this book and smile.

Thank you for joining in.

NOTES

LESSON 1: SEE YOURSELF IN OTHER PEOPLE

p. 26: On 24 May 2006, Mandela gave a TV interview to South African journalist Tim Modise where he explained his understanding of *ubuntu*. It can be viewed at: www.youtube.com/watch?v=ODQ4WiDsEBQ

LESSON 2: STRENGTH LIES IN UNITY

p. 34: In 2012, psychological scientist Cameron Anderson and his colleagues from University of California, Berkeley looked at several studies to conclude socioeconomic status doesn't guarantee a greater sense of well-being: Anderson, C., Kraus, M. W., Galinsky, A. D. and Keltner, D., 'The Local-ladder Effect: Social Status and Subjective Well-being', *Psychological Science*, 20(10), (2012), 1–8.

The 2012 San Francisco Bay Area study, which found that high-status vehicle categories were more likely to commit infractions, was carried out by Paul K. Piff, a then researcher at the Institute of Personality and Social Research at UC Berkeley: Piff, P. K. et al., 'Higher Social Class Predicts Increased Unethical Behavior', *Proceedings of the National Academy of Sciences*, 109, 2012, 4086–91.

p. 35: The 2015 study by Brigham Young University, authored by university researcher Julianne Holt-Lunstad, appeared in the journal *Perspectives on Psychological Science*. Findings revealed loneliness increases the risk of mortality by 26 per cent, and social isolation and living alone increases it by 29 per cent and 32 per cent respectively: Holt-Lunstad, J., 'Loneliness and Social Isolation as Risk Factors for Mortality: A Meta-analytic Review', *Perspectives on Psychological Science*, 10(2) (2015), 227–37.

LESSON 4: CHOOSE TO SEE THE WIDER PERSPECTIVE

p. 66: Tearfund is a Christian relief and development agency and a member of the Disasters Emergency Committee. Founded in 1968, the charity has been working around the world for more than fifty years responding to disasters and helping lift communities out of poverty. For more information about the work of Tearfund, please visit www.tearfund.org

p. 66: Dr Lasana Harris, associate professor of experimental psychology at UCL, conducted research into 'the bystander effect' and how neuroscience can explain the way in which our brains dehumanize others: Harris, L. T. and Fiske, S. T., 'Dehumanizing the Lowest of the Low: Neuroimaging Responses to Extreme Out-groups' in Fiske, S. T., *Social Cognition: Selected Works of Susan T. Fiske* (Routledge, 2018).

p. 68: For over thirty years, Stanford psychologist Carol Dweck has been fascinated by the learning abilities of different students and how some seem crushed by small setbacks while others rebound. She and her team studied the behaviour of thousands of students to form the groundbreaking 'mind-set' thesis: Dweck, C. S., *Mindset* (revised edn, Little, Brown, 2017).

LESSON 5: HAVE DIGNITY AND RESPECT FOR YOURSELF AND OTHERS

p. 77: The World Health Organization believes malnutrition to be one of the most significant threats to human life. Inadequate nutrition but also the rising issue of obesity form a double burden which populations face today, especially in developing countries: www.who.int/nutrition/challenges/en/

p. 78: In the joint study into individualism, the authors were able to examine fifty-one years' worth of data detailing individualist practices and values in seventy-eight countries. Data was drawn from national censuses and overall the results showed a clear pattern. Both individualistic practices and values increased across the globe over time: Santos, H. C., Varnum, M. E. W., and Grossmann, I., 'Global Increases in Individualism', *Psychological Science*, 28(9) 2017, 1228–39.

p. 83: In June 2015, the efforts of CAFOD in halting the spread of Ebola in Sierra Leone were recognized. As part of the World Vision-led SMART consortium – an alliance of faith-based organizations working on the response to the virus – the agency was a recipient of the prestigious BOND International Humanitarian Award. Through training and the provision of equipment, burial workers were able to conduct safe and dignified burials for Ebola victims across the nation: www.cafod.org.uk/News/Press-centre/Press-releases/Ebola-burial-teams-honoured

p. 84: My grandfather's eloquent words on the subject of assisted death appeared in the *Guardian* (12 July 2014): www.theguardian.com/commentisfree/2014/jul/12/desmond-tutu-in-favour-of-assisted-dying

LESSON 6: BELIEVE IN THE GOOD OF EVERYONE

p. 97: More details of Anupurba Saha's heartwarming story and her state-of-the-art blade can be found at: www.bbc.com/news/av/uk-39797685/seven-year-old-returns-to-school-with-prosthetic-aid

p. 101: Christo Brand's story was reported in Andrew Meldrum's article in the *Observer* (20 May 2007): www.theguardian.com/world/2007/may/20/nelsonmandela

p. 102: For further information on the Reticular Activating System (RAS), visit: www.psychologydiscussion.net/brain/functions-of-reticular-activating-system-ras-brain-neurology/2893

LESSON 7: CHOOSE HOPE OVER OPTIMISM

p. 112: The registered charity set up by brothers Magnus and Fergus MacFarlane-Barrow, Mary's Meals, is formally known as Scottish International Relief and sets up feeding programmes in some of the world's poorest communities: www.marysmeals.org.uk. The Scotland Malawi Partnership (SMP) is an umbrella organization with which Mary's Meals works. It exists to coordinate, support and represent Scotland's many civic connections to the African nation. It represents a community of 109,000 people in Scotland with active links there, and a shared history that dates back around 160 years to the travels of Dr David Livingstone. An estimated 44 per cent of Scots can name a friend or family member who has an association with Malawi, making this one of the world's strongest north–south, people-to-people connections.

p. 113: Dr Valerie Maholmes worked at the Yale Child Study Center from 1992 to 2005 and is chief of the Paediatric Trauma and Critical Illness Branch at the Eunice Kennedy Shriver National Institute of Child Health and Human Development (NICHD). She wrote the book *Fostering Resilience and Well-being in Children and Families in Poverty: Why Hope Still Matters* (OUP, 2014), where she discusses research on hope and ways to foster optimism: www.apa.org/monitor/2014/11/hope

p. 114: When Anthony Ray Hinton's conviction was overturned in 2015, he penned his personal story, published as *The Sun Does Shine: How I Found Life and Freedom on Death Row* (St Martin's Press, 2018).

p. 115: Lawyer Bryan Stevenson talks about the importance of hope against great odds in his account of the lives he has defended, *Just Mercy* (Scribe UK, 2015).

LESSON 8: SEEK OUT WAYS TO CONNECT

p. 125: In 2013, researchers from Sweden's Gothenburg University revealed singers in a choir synchronize their heartbeats. Their findings showed that when singers sang in unison their pulses began to speed up and slow down at the same rate: Vickhoff, B. et al., 'Music Structure Determines Heart Rate Variability of Singers', *Frontiers in Psychology*, 4, 2013, 334; www.bbc.co.uk/news/science-environment-23230411

p. 125: In 2000, researchers from University of California, Irvine collected samples of saliva from choral singers to measure immune responses, and their findings revealed a reduction in the stress hormone cortisol and increase in the antibody immunoglobulin A: Beck, R. J. et al., 'Choral Singing, Performance Perception, and Immune System Changes in Salivary Immunoglobulin A and Cortisol', *Music Perception: An Interdisciplinary Journal*, 18(1), 2000, 87–106.

p. 125: Melodic Intonation Therapy (MIT) was the subject of a study on twelve patients at Harvard Medical School whose speech had been impaired by strokes. The patients were taught to sing simple lyrics, which gradually turned into normal speech as their verbal abilities improved. The results suggest the brain can be 'rewired' because the patients with damage to the left side of their brain (responsible for speech) learned to use the right side (associated with singing): Norton, A. et al., 'Melodic Intonation Therapy: Shared Insights on How It Is Done and Why It Might Help', *Annals of the New York Academy of Sciences*, 1169, 2009, 431–6.

For more details on music therapy for stroke patients see: www.saga.co.uk/magazine/health-wellbeing/treatments/complementary-therapies/health-music-therapy

p. 125: A 2012 study from the Department of Experimental Psychology, University of Oxford showed that 'singing, dancing and drumming all trigger endorphin release (indexed by an increase in post-activity pain tolerance) in contexts where merely listening to music and low energy musical activities do not.' Dunbar, R. I., Kaskatis, K., MacDonald, I. and Barra, V., 'Performance of Music Elevates Pain Threshold and Positive Affect: Implications for the Evolutionary Function of Music', *Evolutionary Psychology*, 10(4), 2012, 688–702.

p. 126: A variety of studies has shown that group identification (a sense of belonging to one's social group coupled with a sense of commonality with the group's members) is linked to high levels of satisfaction with life: Wakefield, J. R. H., Sani, F., Madhok, V. et al., 'The Relationship Between Group Identification and Satisfaction with Life in a Cross-cultural Community Sample', *Happiness Studies*, 18, 2017, 785.

p. 126: Sports psychology professor Daniel Wann of Murray State University in Kentucky is the author of the book *Sport Fans: The Psychology and Social Impact of Spectators* (Routledge, 2001). His research programme centred on the psychology of sport fandom, the role of sport in fans' lives, and included several studies such as 'Testing the Team Identification Social-Psychological Health Model: Mediational Relationships Among Team Identification, Sport Fandom, Sense of Belonging, and Meaning in Life', *Group Dynamics: Theory, Research, and Practice*, 21(2), 2017, 94–107.

p. 126: Dr Alan Pringle specializes in mental health nursing at the University of Nottingham and is also quoted as saying that 'football gives families a "common currency" that connects family members unlike few other subjects.' Dr Pringle's words appeared in the article 'How Being a Sports Fan Makes You Happier and Healthier' (*Huffington Post*, 30 January 2015).

p. 130: A much-cited 1984 study by environmental psychologist Roger Ulrich was the first to use the standards of modern medical research – strict experimental controls and quantified health outcomes – to demonstrate that gazing at a garden can sometimes speed healing from surgery, infections and other ailments. Ulrich and his team reviewed the medical records of people recovering from gallbladder surgery at a suburban Pennsylvania hospital. All other things being equal, patients with bedside windows looking out on leafy trees healed, on average, a day faster, needed significantly less pain medication and had fewer postsurgical complications than patients who instead saw a brick wall: Ulrich, R. S., 'View Through a Window May Influence Recovery from Surgery', *Science*, 224(4647), 1984, 420–1.

Almost a decade later, in 1993, Ulrich and his colleagues at Uppsala University Hospital in Sweden randomly assigned 160 heart surgery patients in the intensive care unit to one of six conditions: simulated 'window views' of a large nature photograph (an open, tree-lined stream or a shadowy forest scene); one of two abstract paintings; a white panel; or a blank wall. Patients confirmed afterwards those assigned the water and tree scene were less anxious and needed fewer doses of pain relief than those with a darker forest photo, abstract art or no pictures at all: Ulrich, R.S., Lunden, O. and Etinge, J. L., 'Effects of Exposure to Nature and Abstract Pictures on Patients Recovering from Heart Surgery', Society for Psychophysiological Research, 33rd Annual Meeting, Rottach-Egern, Germany, 30, 1993, S1–S7.

p. 131: The Food Growing in Schools Taskforce Report was published in March 2012 and was led by the charity Garden Organic alongside twenty-five taskforce members, including Morrisons supermarket, the Forestry Commission and the Royal Horticultural Society, and was supported by the Faculty of Public Health: https://betterhealthforall.org/2012/04/03/why-children-benefit-from-growing-their-own-food/

LESSON 9: THE POWER OF THE F-WORD – FORGIVENESS

p. 144: Forgiveness is not just emotionally uplifting, it's good for our health. Studies from Luther College, Iowa, and University of California, Berkeley suggest that 'developing a more forgiving coping style may help minimize stress-related disorders'. Study author Loren Toussaint, an associate professor of psychology at Luther College, found that being highly forgiving erased the link between stress and illness: Toussaint, L., Shields, G. S., Dorn, G. and Slavich, G. M., 'Effects of Lifetime Stress Exposure on Mental and Physical Health in Young Adulthood: How Stress Degrades and Forgiveness Protects Health', *Journal of Health Psychology*, 21(6), 2016, 1004–14.

p. 144: Studies have shown that if a victim of trauma suffering from PTSD (where a perpetrator is to blame) learns to forgive the transgressor, it can have a positive effect on their symptoms:

Cerci, D., and Colucci, E., 'Forgiveness in PTSD After Man-made Traumatic Events: A Systematic Review', *Traumatology*, 24(1) (2018), 47–54.

p. 145: Christophe Mbonyingabo is one of relief agency Tearfund's Inspired Individuals. The programme exists to identify, equip and connect new leaders who are aspiring to live like Jesus and help make their already remarkable ministries as effective as possible. Inspired Individuals are involved in a wide range of efforts – standing up to corruption, working to end trafficking and prostitution, peace-making between divided peoples and offering new hope to street children: www.tearfund.org/en/inspired_individuals

LESSON 10: EMBRACE OUR DIVERSITY

p. 156: The 2018 report published by the Royal Society for Public Health in partnership with the Calouste Gulbenkian Foundation revealed the extent of ageist attitudes across the UK, and how they harm the health and well-being of everyone in society as we grow older: www.rsph.org.uk/about-us/news/a-quarter-of-millennials-believe-depression-normal-in-older-age.html

p. 157: For further details on the research that reveals when we see others being harmed – even complete strangers – the same part of our brain is stimulated as if we were being harmed ourselves, see: www.psychologicalscience.org/observer/i-feel-your-pain-the-neuroscience-of-empathy

p. 162: More information about Eleanor Riley's registered charity, Made With Hope, can be found at: www.madewithhope.org

LESSON 12: FIND HUMOUR IN OUR HUMANITY

p. 188: The study that reveals humans have evolved to laugh was conducted by the Department of Psychiatry, Osaka University Graduate School of Medicine, Suita, Japan: Takeda, M. et al., 'Laughter and Humor as Complementary and Alternative Medicines for Dementia Patients', *BMC Complementary and Alternative Medicine*, 10, 2010, 28; http://mentalfloss.com/article/539632/scientific-benefits-having-laugh

p. 193: A sense of humour helps to keep people healthy and increases their chances of reaching retirement age. But after the age of seventy, the health benefits of humour decrease, researchers at the Norwegian University of Science and Technology (NTNU) have found.

The 2010 study has been published in the *International Journal of Psychiatry in Medicine*, and was composed of an examination of records from 53,500 individuals who were followed up after seven years. The study is based on a comprehensive database from the second Nor-Trøndelag Health Study, called HUNT-2, which is comprised of health histories and blood samples collected between 1995 and 1997 from more than 70,000 residents of a county in mid-Norway: Svebak, S., Romundstad, S. and Holmen, J., 'A 7-year Prospective Study of Sense of Humor and Mortality in an Adult County Population: The HUNT-2 Study', *International Journal of Psychiatry in Medicine*, 40(2), 2010, 125–46.

LESSON 13: WHY LITTLE THINGS MAKE A BIG DIFFERENCE

p. 203: UK Giving is the largest study of giving behaviour in the UK. The latest report interviewed over 12,000 people across the UK, allowing us to look in more detail than ever before at patterns of giving: www.cafonline.org/about-us/publications/2018 publications/uk giving report 2010, www.neoncrm.com/10-year-end-giving-statistics-every-fundraiser-should-know, https://nonprofitssource.com/online-giving-statistics/#Online

p. 204: The researchers from Uppsala University, Sweden who investigated how seeing other people smile suppresses the control we have over our own smile found that 'according to the facial feedback hypothesis, facial muscles do not only express emotions, they also have the ability to modulate subjective experiences of emotions and to initiate emotions.': Dimberg, U., and Söderkvist, S. J., 'The Voluntary Facial Action Technique: A Method to Test the Facial Feedback Hypothesis', *Journal of Nonverbal Behavior*, 35, 2011, 17.

p. 205: More information on the 2013 study which showed a correlation between the use of first-person singular pronouns and mental health problems can be found at: www.thisisreallyinteresting.com/talking-a-lot-about-yourself-a-sign-of-distress. Zimmermann, J., Wolf, M., Bock, A., Peham, D. and Benecke, C., 'The Way We Refer to Ourselves Reflects How We Relate to Others: Associations Between First-person Pronoun Use and Interpersonal Problems', *Journal of Research in Personality*, 47(3), 2013, 218–25.

ACKNOWLEDGEMENTS

I have to start by thanking my mother, Naomi, who has always had faith in me, most importantly when I have not. To this day I still seek her guidance and this endeavour was no different. I am sure she will be relieved to be free of my constant calls and texts begging her to edit something for me, but I could not have done it without her. I am a very lucky daughter. Thank you.

None of this would have been possible without my partner, Edd, who was my cheerleader alongside my mother and happily supported me not only emotionally during this journey but also financially. He never complained and never doubted me. Thank you for being you, you teach me every day.

To my grandfather, thank you for agreeing to write a foreword for your granddaughter who sometimes teases you.

Special and never-ending thanks to Shannon Kyle for her invaluable help in the writing of this book. I'll be anxiously awaiting your book now.

To Andrea Henry, my editor at Transworld, who took a chance and brought this book idea to me. Thank you, because none of us would be here without you. I am thankful for your insight and understanding nature. I feel like I hit the editor jackpot.

To my agent, Piers Blofeld. Thank you for patiently putting up with a young and inexperienced author who had *all* the questions, and for always giving the story to me straight.

To Lynn Franklin, though you have stepped away from the literary world, I know you gave me as much guidance and support as you did my grandfather when he was writing his books. Thank you for all the emails, texts and calls.

To my copy-editor, Rebecca Wright. I don't know how you do it, but thank you for the magic you work.

To Ann-Katrin Ziser, Josh Crosley and Helen Edwards at Transworld. Thank you for fighting my corner. And to the rest of the Transworld team – especially Hannah Bright in Publicity, Alice Murphy-Pyle in Marketing, and Marianne Issa El-Khoury, who designed the cover artwork. Thank you so much for your hard work.

Thanks also to Hampton for the amazing page design.

To Marsha and Randy, thank you for your willingness to edit anything and everything. And thanks to the storyteller Robert Pierre, who helped me in the very beginning to find ways to get words and thoughts on the page.

To my friends and family in South Africa, the US and the UK. Thank you for being my hype people. Thanks to Maggie Conner Finn and Marianna Weaver for moonlighting as photographers when I was in need.

And to Clive Conway and the Tutu Foundation UK, who have done such great work in my grandfather's name and allowed us to share it in the book, as well as Joseph Duncan and Youth Futures. Thank you.

Last, but certainly not least, to all the people who agreed to be interviewed. I know seeing your name and story down on paper can be different than expected, so thank you for sharing your stories.

I apologize to those I may not have thanked by name, and hope you know that I am grateful for the work you put in to making this book happen.